TABLE OF CONTENTS

Ask your friends and family to join you in 'Hands On' crafting fun and you'll soon see how easy it is to double the fun and creativity when you're crafting together...

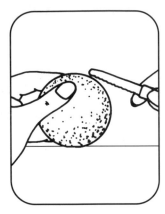

1. Styrofoam can be cut easily by rubbing the edge of a plastic knife with an old wax candle. Cut through the foam with a sawing motion. Use a scrap piece of the Styrofoam to 'sand' any rough edges.

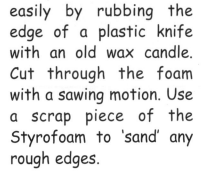

2. **IMPORTANT!** When you see the 'helping hand' symbol on a project page, it means you may need adult supervision to do the project. Always use care when using tools or a heat source. Be careful and safe!

3. Trace the patterns as needed onto the tracing paper. Lay the traced pattern on top of project surface. Place transfer, or graphite paper under the pattern then trace over design with a soft pencil, or crayon.

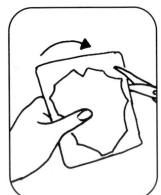

4. When cutting with a pair of scissors always work slowly and evenly. Hold the material you are cutting with the opposite hand, turning it toward the scissors as you cut.

5. When painting or working with messy materials, don't forget to protect your work surface with plastic or newspaper and your clothes with an apron or old shirt. Keep a roll of paper towels handy to wipe up spills.

Waxed Paper

6. To make sure paint doesn't seep through the shirts or fabric, use a piece of cardboard or wax paper inside the shirt or under fabric while painting. Tape the sleeves and excess shirt together at the back of the board.

7. There are some basic supplies that are used throughout the book which are not always in the project supply list. Some of these general supplies are: paper clips, toothpicks, paper, tracing paper etc.

8. For best results, always read and follow directions given on each product label. Some products may seem to do the same thing, but there may be important differences you need to know.

TRADITIONS

- Foam Quilt Block
- Decorated Candles
- Woven Heart
- Brown Bag Appliqué Cat
- Functional Family
- Apple Dolls

Foam Quilt Block

by Jennie McGuffee

Who says quilting is just with fabric! Arrange colored squares of foam to make interesting patterns and a great door sign for your room.

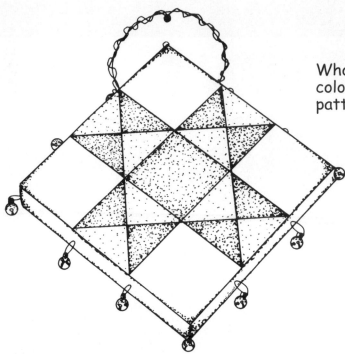

You will need:
6" x 6" x 1" Piece of Styrofoam
3 Foam sheets - Green, Yellow and Purple
Scissors
Tacky Glue
12 Paper clips
11 Silver bells

1. Cut a 6" x 6" piece of green foam and glue it to the top of the styrofoam sheet.

2. Cut four 2" x 2" squares of yellow foam and glue one square to each corner on top of the green foam.

3. Cut three 2" x 2" squares of purple foam. Glue one of the squares to the center top of the green foam. Cut the remaining squares diagonally into four pieces to form triangles. Glue the triangles in place as shown on the diagram.

4. Cut four 1" x 6" strips of yellow foam and glue them around the sides of the styrofoam.

5. Unbend the paper clips. Push one through the yellow foam at the top corner for a hanger. Place a silver bell on the large end of each paper clip, squeeze together then push the smaller end through the yellow foam into the side of the quilt. There should be a bell on three corners and two bells on each side of the quilt.

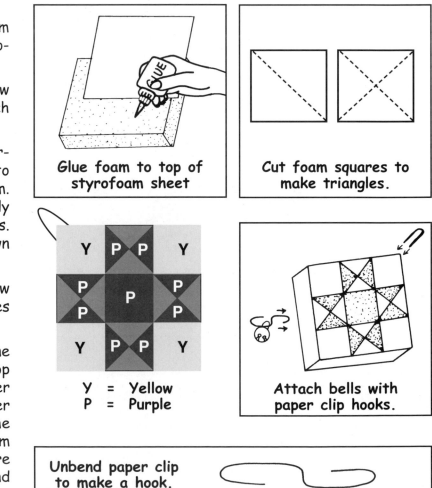

Glue foam to top of styrofoam sheet

Cut foam squares to make triangles.

Y	P	P	Y
P	P		P
P		P	
	P		P
Y	P	P	Y

Y = Yellow
P = Purple

Attach bells with paper clip hooks.

Unbend paper clip to make a hook.

Darice® Foamies™ and Bells; Elmer's® Craftbond™ Tacky Glue; Fiskars® Student Scissors and Ruler; Dow Styrofoam® Brand Plastic Foam

Decorated Candles
by Tracia Ledford Williams

See how much fun you can have and how many different candle designs you and your friends can create from our patterns.

You will need:
Gold and Silver foil
Foil Adhesive and Sealer
Compressed sponge
Scissors
#12 Brush
Assorted pillar candles

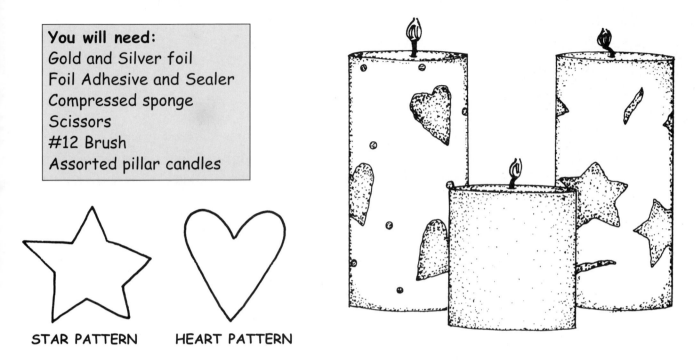

STAR PATTERN   HEART PATTERN

1. Transfer shapes onto compressed sponge and cut out. Wet sponge to expand then wring out excess water.

2. Pour a 3" puddle of adhesive onto a paper plate. Dip sponge shape into the adhesive then press on candle. Make dots and lines by dipping the paintbrush or the handle in adhesive and pressing against candle. Allow the adhesive to dry clear.

3. Cut a piece of foil and press shiny side up against the dried adhesive on the candle. The foil will stick to the adhesive.

4. To cover the entire candle with foil, use a scruffy brush and paint the entire candle with adhesive. When the adhesive dries clear, apply the foil.

Cut shapes from compressed sponge.

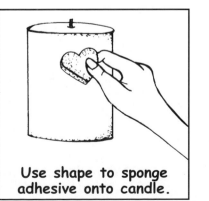

Use shape to sponge adhesive onto candle.

Press foil (shiny side up) onto dried adhesive.

Delta Renaissance Foil™; Eagle® #12 Golden Taklon Brush; Fiskars® Scissors.

You've Woven My Heart
by Julie McGuffee

Use this simple weaving technique to make a woven heart into a pocket heart.

You will need:	Scissors
Two tone paper, or Dark	Heart punch
Pink and Lt. Pink paper	Small bow (optional)
Decorative scissors	Glue

1. Trace the pattern onto tag board. Fold colored paper in half then place the pattern on the paper with the straight edge against the fold. Cut two patterns from colored paper then cut along the inside pattern lines with plain or decorative scissors.

2. Turn one piece of paper the opposite way around, so that a different color shows on the outside.

3. Lay one pattern piece on top of the other pattern piece. Weave the top loop through and around the loops on the opposite pattern piece. Continue weaving the loops through and around until both pieces are woven together.

4. Cut a 1" x 8" piece of paper for a handle. Cut a second piece a little narrower with decorative scissors then glue the second piece on top of the first with the opposite color facing upwards. Glue the ends inside the heart.

5. Use the punch to cut small heart shapes from the same paper then glue to the front of the heart as shown.

PLACE ON FOLD

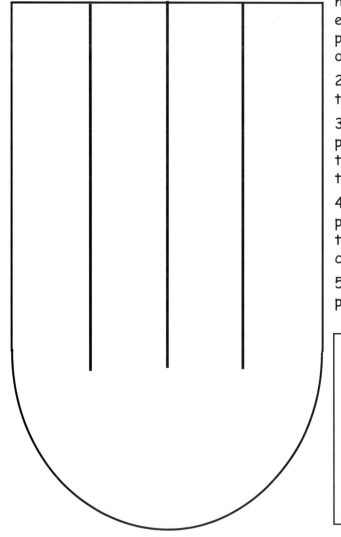

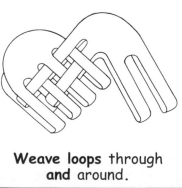

Weave loops through **and** around.

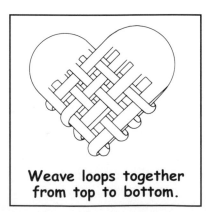

Weave loops together from top to bottom.

Bemiss-Jason Fadeless Duet® Paper;
Fiskars® Paper Edgers®, Scissors & Heart Punch; Elmer's® White School Glue

You will need:

7" x 10" Corrugated Natural paper
6 ¾" x 9 ¾" White construction paper
3 ½" x 5 ½" Off White construction paper
Two 6" x 6" Brown construction paper
Two ½" wood buttons
Black embroidery floss
Two Black E-beads
Fiberfill or cotton
One ¼" Pink and two ⅜" White pompoms
Fabric scraps
Raffia
White glue
Paper punch
Large eye sharp needle
Scissors and decorative edge scissors

1. Cut 36" of black embroidery floss. To separate the floss, place three strands in each hand and pull apart slowly, letting them untwist. Thread one end of the floss through the needle and tie a knot in the other end. Trace the cat pattern onto brown paper.
2. Holding two pieces of brown paper together, cut around cat pattern.
3. Starting from the back of paper layers, blanket stitch around the cat shape as shown in diagram. Leave a 2" opening and stuff the cat lightly with fiberfil. Finish stitching.
4. Make straight stitches at center front for legs.
5. Sew, or glue buttons to bottom of legs for paws. Sew or glue two E-beads on face for eyes. Glue pom-pom nose and cheeks below eyes.
6. Hold the corrugated paper with the ridges running from top to bottom. Fold in half then cut along the fold to make the back and the front of the card.
7. Trim the edge of the off-white paper with decorative scissors then glue to the center front of card. Use remaining strands of floss to make straight stitches ¼" from the edge of the off-white construction paper.
8. Glue the cat to center front of the card. Cut out fabric patches and glue them in place on card front.
9. Fold white paper in half and place between front and back pieces of card. Punch 5 holes along the left side of card then thread raffia through them. Tie a bow at the top to finish.

Brown Bag Appliqué Cat
by Patty Cox
This project is just purr-fect!

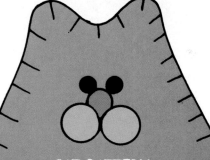

CAT PATTERN

RUNNING STITCH

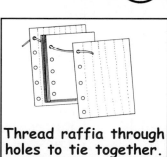

Thread raffia through holes to tie together.

BLANKET STITCH

Bemiss-Jason Corobuff® and Spectra® Construction Paper; Darice® Wood Buttons, Raffia, and Pompoms; Elmer's® White School Glue; Fiskars® Student Scissors and Paper Edgers.

Functional Family
by Patty Cox

A system of interlocking gears makes a perfect family wall hanging that illustrates working together.

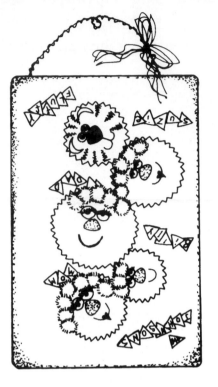

PET EAR
PATTERN

You will need:
3mm Foam sheet in your
  family's skin color
Metal compass
Pinking shears
15 mm Shank noses
Wiggle eyes
Pompoms (for hair)
5" x 9" Foam board (add 4" to length
  for each extra circle over 5)
Fine tipped markers
Triangle hole punch
Construction paper

1. Use a compass to draw 2" circles on selected flesh-tone foam. Make one circle for each member of your family. Cut out each circle with pinking shears. **Note:** Trim the edges of the circle until full points meet. Half points will not connect and turn the gears.
2. Enlarge the hole in the center of the circle (marked by the point of the compass) with a toothpick or pencil point.
3. Cut a base from foam core about 5" x 9". This will be large enough for 5 circles. Arrange the foam wheels on board as shown.
4. Firmly press wheels together so all of their gears connect tightly. To mark circle centers on foam core, poke sharp end of compass through foam core to make hole. Enlarge the hole.
5. Secure gears to board with 15mm shank noses. Press nose post through hole in the foam circle and board. Use pink or brown noses for people faces and a black nose for a pet's face. Glue wiggle eyes on all faces and pompom hair. Draw a half circle mouth using a fine tipped red marker. Cut pet ears and insert into slits on each side of head.
6. Punch triangles for letters from construction paper and glue onto the board. Write names on triangles with marker.

Use a compass
to draw circles

Cut circles with pinking
(zig-zag edge) shears.

Position circles so that
the edges interlock.

Fiskars® Metal Compass, Paper Edgers, Scissors and Hole Punch; Darice® Foamies™, Wiggle Eyes, Shank Noses and Pompoms; Bemiss-Jason Construction Paper

Shrunken Apple Dolls

project provided courtesy of FamilyFun Magazine

Not just for keeping the doctor away - use apples to make appealing craft projects!

You will need:
Red or golden delicious apple
½ cup Lemon juice
1 tblsp. Salt
Potato peeler or knife
Cloves and rice
Large paintbrush
Glue

1. Peel a large apple (red or golden delicious work best).
2. Coat the apple with a mixture of $\frac{1}{3}$ cup lemon juice and one tablespoon of salt.
3. Use a potato peeler or knife to carve eye sockets, nose, mouth and ears.
4. Stick in cloves for eyes and rice for teeth.
5. Place the apple on a bottle cap or drying rack in a warm, dry place for about two weeks. Shape the face as it shrinks and hardens.
6. To make dolls, place a cork in the opening of an empty plastic soda bottle. Attach the head to the cork then drape the bottle with fabric for clothing. Add yarn for hair.

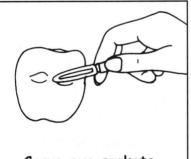

Coat apple with lemon juice and salt

Carve eye sockets, nose and mouth.

Add clove eyes, rice teeth and yarn hair.

FamilyFun Magazine - 1(800)248-4849/www.familyfun.com;
Elmer's® Craftbond Tacky Glue

FALL INTO CRAFTS

- Creepy Bugs
- Oak Leaf Frame
- Pine Cone Repoussé
- Pony Bead Corn Cob
- Handprint Wreath
- Fall Banner

Creepy Bug

by Dimensions Perler Beads

Have fun making a whole family of creepy spiders in a variety of glow in the dark colors.

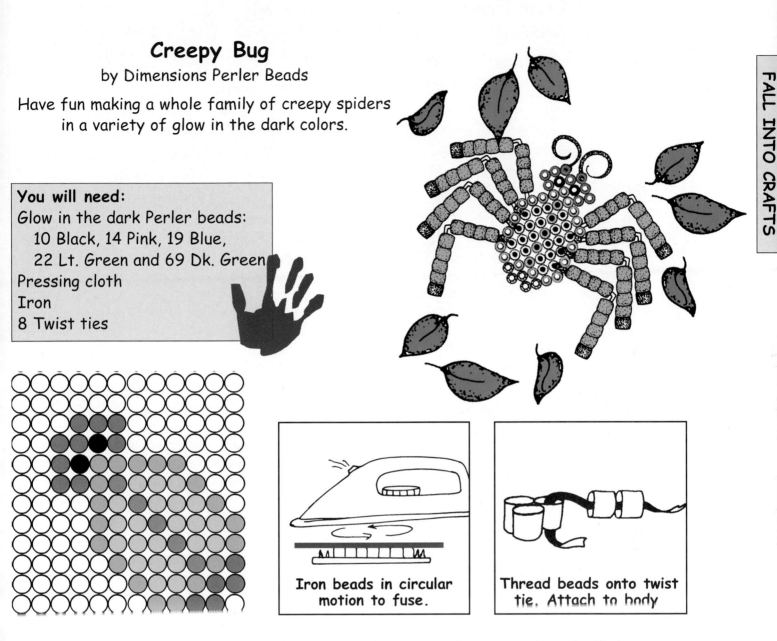

You will need:
Glow in the dark Perler beads:
    10 Black, 14 Pink, 19 Blue,
    22 Lt. Green and 69 Dk. Green
Pressing cloth
Iron
8 Twist ties

Iron beads in circular motion to fuse.

Thread beads onto twist tie. Attach to body

1. Working on a flat surface, create your design by placing beads one by one on a pegboard. Follow our patterns or be creative and design your own.

2. **Ask an adult** to preheat a dry household iron to the medium setting. When carrying the bead design to the iron, be careful not to tip or bump the beads from the pegboard! Cover the beads with the ironing paper. Keeping the iron level, gently iron the beads in a circular motion for about 30 seconds to fuse the beads evenly.

3. Once the design is cool, peel off the ironing paper. Lift your design from the pegboard and flip it over onto your ironing surface.

4. Cover with the ironing paper then iron the other side to fuse it evenly.

5. To make spider legs, thread about 8 perler beads on each black twist tie. Thread one end of the tie through the hole in a bead on the side of the body. Twist the opposite end to hold the beads in place.

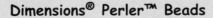

Dimensions® Perler™ Beads

Oak Leaf Frame
by Brenda Spitzer

Find a pile of leaves, and when you're finished jumping in them, save a few to make a molded plaster frame.

You will need:
9 ⅞" × 11 ⅞" × ¾" Styrofoam sheet
6-8 Preserved or fresh oak leaves
8oz. White school glue
1 Cup of Plaster of Paris
1 Tbsp. sand (your choice of color)
1 Tbsp. Beige acrylic paint
10" Wall board knife (or putty knife)
Transparent Acrylic paint - Yellow,
    Green, Lt. Brown and Brick Red
Matte varnish
Paint brush
Ruler
Pencil
Petroleum jelly
Drop cloth

1. Gather leaves for your frame.

2. Mark an opening in the center of the styrofoam 2½" from all outer edges then cut out the center opening with a plastic knife. (Fig. 1). Cut from the front to the back.

3. Mix 8 oz. of Elmers glue with one cup plaster of Paris, 1 tablespoon of sand and 1 tablespoon of beige acrylic paint in a plastic container. **Hint:** This step is messy - work outside if possible.

4. Cover your work surface with a plastic drop cloth. Use a putty knife to spread the plaster mixture ¼" thick over the front, inside and outside edges of the styrofoam frame. (Fig. 2) Run a wallboard knife over the front of the frame to make the surface as smooth as possible. Allow to set for 10 minutes.

4. Lightly coat the back of the leaves with petroleum jelly. Position the leaves on the front of the frame and press gently with your fingers. Use the handle of a paintbrush to press down the tips and edges of the leaves. (Fig. 3). Allow to dry for about 30 minutes.

6. Pick up the end of the stem with tweezers and gently lift off the leaves. **Note:** If leaves do not release easily, press them back in place and let them dry for another 15 minutes before trying to lift them again. When all the leaves have been removed, allow the frame to dry hard.

7. Apply transparent acrylic paints to leaf impressions with a small paint brush. Gently wipe painted areas with a paper towel.

8. Apply matte varnish to painted areas.

Clean Up Tips: Putty and wallboard knives can be scraped clean once they are dry. The dry plaster mixture will pop out of a plastic container by flexing the sides. Clean brushes with soap and water.

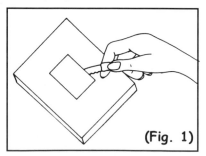

(Fig. 1)

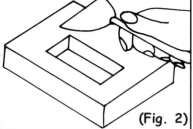

(Fig. 2)

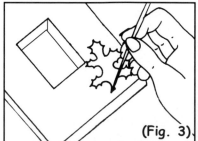

(Fig. 3)

Elmer's® Washable School Glue; Delta Ceramcoat® Acrylic Paint, Ceramcoat® Soft Tints and Matte Varnish; Dow Styrofoam® Brand Plastic Foam; Eagle Paint Brushes

Pine Cone Repoussé
by Patty Cox

No need to despair if there are no pine trees in your area, it's easy to make your own pine cones!

You will need:
3" Styrofoam egg
Tacky Glue
12" x 12" aluminum foil
Media mixer
Green raffia
Dried Lima Beans
Acrylic paint - Brown,
    Metallic Gold, and
    Metallic Green
Plastic knife
Natural paper, handle bag

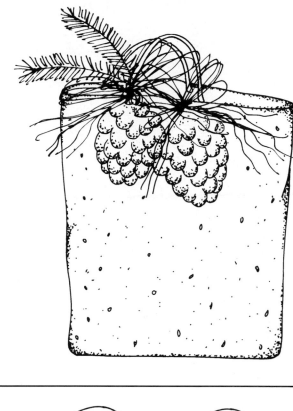

1. Cut styrofoam egg in half lengthwise with a plastic knife.

2. Apply tacky glue to small end of egg then press a dried lima bean halfway into styrofoam at the tip of the egg.

3. Apply glue to next row. Insert about 8 rows of lima beans, offsetting bean scallops on each row as shown in the diagram. Allow glue to set.

4. Tear a 12" square of aluminum foil. Crumple the foil then carefully reopen it.

5. Place the pine cone on a flat surface then put the foil on top of the pine cone. Starting in the center of the pine cone, gently press the foil into the spaces between the beans. Work out toward the edges, being careful not to tear the foil. Trim the foil and wrap the edges at the back of the pine cone.

6. Squeeze brown and metallic gold paint and a puddle of media mixer onto a paint palette. Use a scrap of foil as a paint palette. First dip your brush in media mixer then in the paint. Paint the pine cone then wipe off the raised areas with a paper towel. Let dry.

7. Push a sharp pencil through the top of the pine cone. Thread strands of raffia through the hole. Tie raffia in a bow.

To make a gift bag: Dip an old toothbrush into green metallic paint, then spatter a paper handle bag. Let dry then tie the pine cones to the bag handles with raffia.

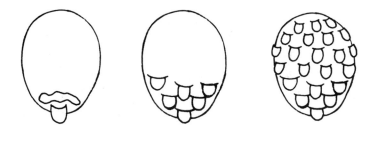

Starting at the tip, glue rows of lima beans into the styrofoam egg.

Cover with foil.

Paint over foil with metallic paint.

Dow Styrofoam® Brand Plastic Foam; Elmer's® Craftbond™ Tacky Glue; Darice® Satin Raffia; Delta Ceramcoat® Acrylic Paints; Bemiss-Jason Kraft™ Handle Bag

Pony Bead Corn Cob
by Patty Cox

Make your own corn for holiday decorations. With the help of your family and friends, you'll be able to decorate every room in the house!

You will need:

3" Styrofoam egg
112 Opaque pony beads: Yellow, Red, Orange, Brown, Black, and White
Natural straw raffia
Yellow crêpe paper
White glue
Straight pins
Pencil

CORN HUSK PATTERN

CUT 7

1. Push a pencil vertically all the way through the center of a styrofoam egg. Reduce the width of the egg by rolling it on a table top. Remove the pencil.

2. Cut nine, 20" long strands of straw raffia and thread them all through the center hole in the egg.

3. Thread 12 assorted color pony beads on one raffia strand. Tug on the beaded strand to find the other end. Tie the two ends together at the top of the egg. Secure the strand to the sides of the egg with two straight pins. Push the pins through the raffia into the styrofoam. Thread 13 beads on the next strand. Tie the ends together at the top of the egg and secure it next to the first strand with straight pins. Keep threading strands of 12 and 13 beads alternately. Tie them together at the top keeping the rows next to each other with straight pins. The bead strands should cover the front half of the egg.

4. Cut seven corn husks from yellow crêpe paper. Pinch the bottom ends of the husks together. Glue the pinched ends of the husks into the bottom hole of the styrofoam egg.

5. Spread glue over the back of the styrofoam egg and pull up a husk to cover it. Bring up one husk at a time and glue it in place on the back of the egg. Tie all the husks together with raffia at the top of the egg.

6. To make a gift bag, tie two of the raffia strands together on the handle of a gift bag and fill the bag with popcorn!

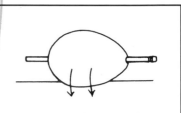
Roll the egg to make smaller and flatter.

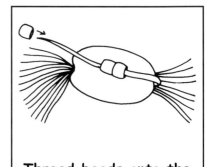
Thread beads onto the raffia strands.

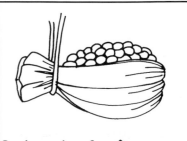
Push ends of crêpe paper husks into egg bottom then tie at the top.

Hand Print Wreath
by Jennie McGuffee

Make a wreath of thank you's filled with all the things you or your whole group of friends are thankful for.

You will need:
12" Styrofoam wreath
Assorted metallic papers
Assorted decorative papers
Black marker
Raffia
Colored craft sticks
Glue
Scissors

1. Make a hand pattern by drawing around your own hand or use the pattern given. Trace patterns on to tag board then cut out.

2. Trace around pattern then cut 6 each green, yellow, red and brown waffle paper hands. Cut 2 each silver and gold and 3 copper hands from metallic corrugated paper. **Note:** Trace pattern onto back of corrugated paper.

3. Starting at the outer edge of the styrofoam wreath, glue one row of hands around the edge in the following order: red, yellow, green and brown. Glue a second row of hands around the inside edge of the wreath. Glue a third row of hands in metallic colors on top of the first two rows in the following order: silver, copper and gold. Carefully push the colored craft sticks into the outer edge of the wreath.

4 Write the names of friends and family or other things you are thankful for on the hands, or clip special photographs to the craft sticks with mini clothespins.

HAND PATTERN

Used with Permission
Accu-Cut®
Roller Die
Cutting Systems

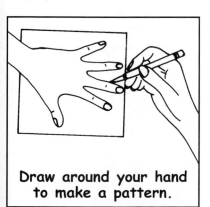
Draw around your hand to make a pattern.

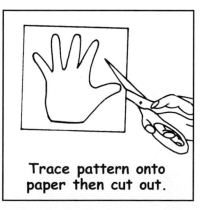
Trace pattern onto paper then cut out.

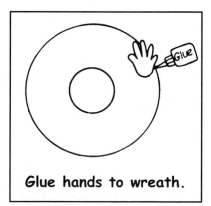
Glue hands to wreath.

Elmer's® White School Glue; Forster® Craft Sticks; Accu-Cut® Die Cut Shapes; Bemiss-Jason® Waffle Paper, Corobuff™ Metallic Sheets; Fiskars® Scissors

Fall Banner
by Tracia Ledford Williams

Announce the seasons with a painted banner for your home or room.

You will need:
Acrylic paint - Yellow, Green, Orange
Textile Medium
#8 Flat brush
13 ½" dowel
2 Small wood candle cups or spools
Tracing and transfer paper
Fabric and wood glue
Cardboard and masking tape
Orange raffia
Iron
Black fabric pen

1. Cut a piece of heavy duty muslin 24" long by 14½" wide. Have a parent help you fold under 1" all around and iron it down. Secure the folds to the back of the muslin with fabric glue.

2. Turn the top edge of the banner under one more inch and glue only at the edge. This will make a casing for the dowel hanger.

3. Tape the banner to cardboard with masking tape.

4. Trace over the pattern with tracing paper. Place a sheet of transfer paper under the tracing paper. Transfer the pattern onto the banner. Refer to the sample photo for placement of the pieces. Go back over the pattern with a black permanent pen.

5. Mix the colors with textile medium before using. Paint leaves with a combination of orange, yellow and green. Blend colors together while they are wet to achieve new colors. Paint the letters on the banner as follows:

   W-yellow, **E**-orange, **L**-green, **C**-yellow,
   O-orange, **M**-green, **E**-yellow.

6. Let all paint dry. Heat set according to directions on the textile medium. (You may need an adult to help you do this.)

7. Paint the dowel and candle cups orange. Let dry. Slip dowel through casing in top of banner. Glue spools or candle cups to ends of dowel.

8. Cut several pieces of raffia 36" long. Twist the ends together and tie them at each end of the dowel to make the hanger. Tie a simple raffia bow and glue it to one side of the banner.

Transfer patterns onto muslin banner.

Use an iron to heat set textile paint.

Glue spools or candle cups to ends of dowels.

Delta Ceramcoat® Acrylic Paint and Textile Medium; Eagle® Brushes; Darice® Wood Spools and Raffia; Elmers® Wood Glue and Fabric Glue

MOSAICS

- Mosaic Tiles
- Mosaic Box
- Many Faceted Mosaic Frame
- Butterfly Mosaic
- Mosaic Keepsake Box
- Clay Pot Mosaic

Mosaic Tile
by Patty Cox

Add a splash of color to a kitchen or patio with a decorated tile.

You will need:
4¼" Ceramic tile
Carbon Paper
Masking tape

Marker
Colored glue pens:
Yellow, Blue, Green,
Purple. Red, and Pink

1. Trace the pattern onto tracing paper. Tape the tracing paper to the tile, aligning edges then slide carbon paper under the pattern. Trace over pattern lines with a ball point pen to transfer pattern to the tile. Remove tape and pattern.

2. Outline pattern lines with colored glue then, starting at the widest part of the design, fill in the center. Work from the center of the tile outwards, to avoid smudging. Use a toothpick to stir out bubbles and evenly fill in each design area. Let dry.

Hint: Speed up drying time by placing your tile outside on a warm day.

TILE PATTERN - ACTUAL SIZE

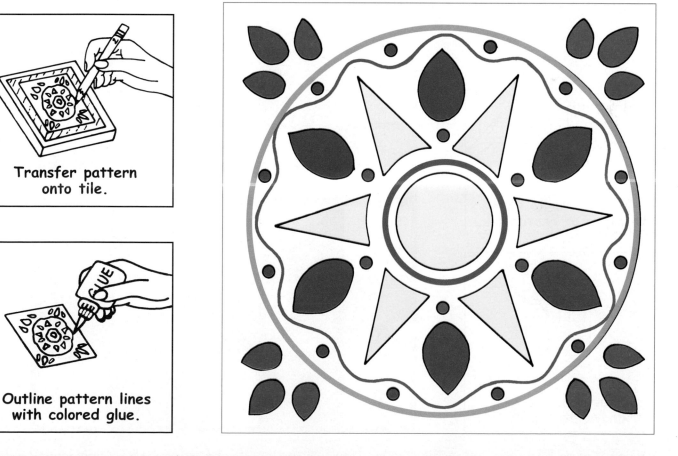

Transfer pattern onto tile.

Outline pattern lines with colored glue.

Elmer's® Squeeze Creations™ Squeeze Pens

Mosaic Box
by Jennie McGuffee

Arrange bits of paper into an attractive mosaic pattern to decorate boxes for a gift, or your own treasures.

You will need:

6" Square paper maché box	Metallic paper - Silver, Green, Blue and Pink
Black acrylic or paper paint	Glue stick
Gloss découpage sealer	Paintbrush
	Scissors

1. Paint the lid and sides of the box black. Let dry.
2. Cut metallic paper into 1" squares as follows: silver-13 (**S**), pink-6 (**P**), blue-8 (**B**) and green-8 (**G**).
3. Cut 2 pink and 2 blue squares in half diagonally to form triangles. Cut 6 blue and 4 pink squares in half across the center to form rectangles.
4. Referring to the diagram, glue the squares and triangles in place on the lid. Glue pink and blue rectangles around the edge of the lid. Let dry.
5. Paint the lid with gloss decoupage sealer to finish.

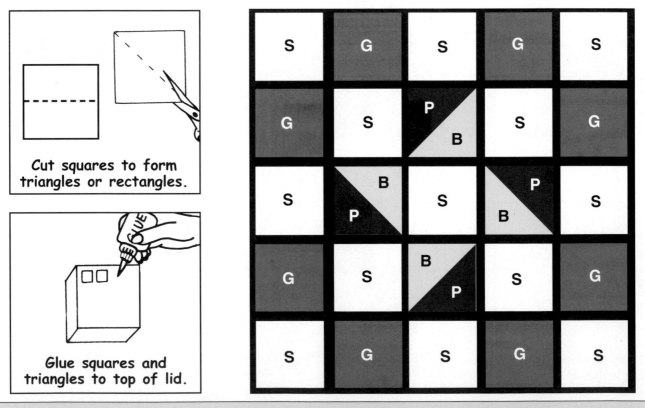

Cut squares to form triangles or rectangles.

Glue squares and triangles to top of lid.

Bemiss-Jason Fadeless® Metallic Paper; Darice® Papier Maché Box; Delta Ceramcoat® Acrylic or Cherished Memories™ Paper Paint; Elmer's® Gel Glue Stick and Gloss Decoupage Sealer; Fiskars® Student Scissors, 12" Ruler; Eagle® Golden Taklon Brush

Many Faceted Mosaic Frame
by Julie McGuffee

Display precious family photos, or photos of friends in special beaded, mosaic frames.

You will need:

5" x 7" Photo mat, poster board, or craft frame
8mm Faceted beads: Purple, Blue, Pink and Yellow
Tacky Glue
4 White chenille stems
Scissors

1. Thread purple beads onto a chenille stem until it is long enough to glue along the outer edge of the frame on one side. Glue in place. Repeat for the rest of the outside and inside edges of the frame.

2. Referring to the diagram, glue the blue, pink and yellow beads in the space between the rows of purple beads.

Thread beads onto chenille stems.

Glue stems around edges of frame.

Glue beads in place following pattern as shown, or design your own.

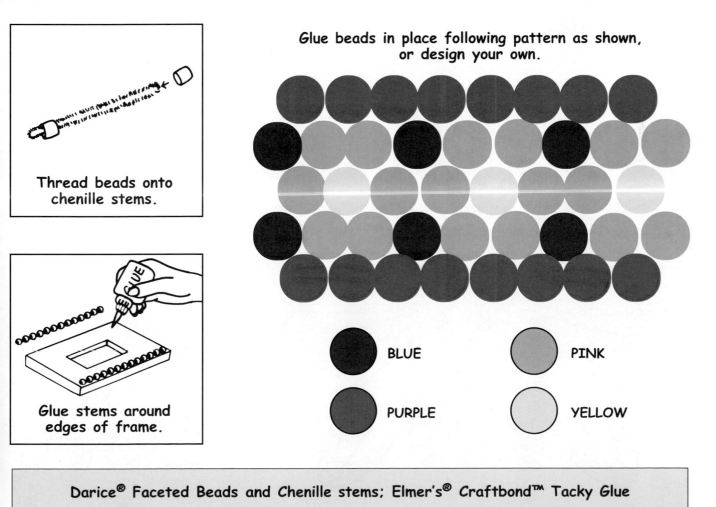

BLUE

PINK

PURPLE

YELLOW

Darice® Faceted Beads and Chenille stems; Elmer's® Craftbond™ Tacky Glue

Butterfly Mosaic
by Brenda Spitzer

Butterflies are mosaics of flying colors. See how their wings are made up of different shapes and colors.

You will need:	
9" x 12" White tag board	Glue Stick
Yellow crayon	Scissors
Watercolor paints	Paint brush
12" x 18" waffle paper	Ruler
	Pencil

1. Divide the tag board into three 4$\frac{1}{2}$" x 6" sections.

2. Using butterfly designs for inspiration, draw or trace the outline of a butterfly onto the tag board with yellow crayon. Fill in sections of the butterfly with different designs, using combinations of lines, ovals, teardrops and circles.

3. Use watercolors to paint brightly colored stripes over the butterfly. The design of the yellow crayon will resist the paint and show through while the paper absorbs the paint. Draw and paint different butterflies on two more pieces of tag board. Let dry.

4. Cut an 8" x 18" piece of waffle paper. Center then glue butterflies in a row on the waffle paper with a glue stick.

Create fabulous butterfly designs by combining oval, circles and teardrop shapes. The body is made up of two ovals with small circles representing the head. See how creative you can be and design a butterfly of your own!

Bemiss-Jason Tag board and Spectra® Waffle Paper;
Elmer's® Washable School Glue Stick; Fiskars® Scissors, Ruler and Watercolors

Mosaic Keepsake Box

by Tracia Ledford Williams

Cut out geometric shapes then use them in a unique way to make a painted mosaic box.

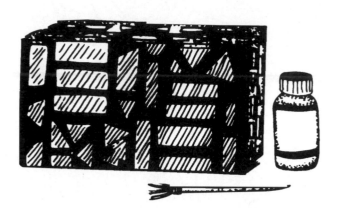

You will need:
Cardboard or paper maché box
Satin découpage medium
Black and white paper paint
Poster board
Assorted colored tissue paper
Decorative edge scissors
Scissors
3/4" Flat brush
#5 Round brush
Old toothbrush

1. Use the flat brush to paint the box white then set aside to dry.

2. Cut small pieces of tissue paper with decorative scissors.

3. Paint an even coat of decoupage medium on a 4" x 4" area of the box. Use your fingers to place the tissue pieces over the decoupage medium. Try overlapping pieces to create new colors. Cover the whole box this way. Let dry.

4. Cut the poster board into assorted small squares, rectangles and triangles. Arrange the posterboard shapes on one side of the box leaving a 1/4" space between the pieces.

5. (You may want to wear rubber gloves for this step!) Dip the toothbrush into black paint then drag your thumb over the bristles to spatter the area between the shapes. Let paint dry. Move the posterboard shapes to another side of the box and repeat. Spatter the whole box in this manner.

6. Dip the #5 round brush in black paint and paint in all the areas that are spattered. The solid black lines around the colored shapes create the mosaic effect.

7. Paint three coats of decoupage medium on your box to seal. Allow each coat to dry between applications.

Glue colored tissue paper to the box.

Arrange posterboard shapes on box then spatter.

Brush with 3 coats of decoupage medium.

Delta Cherished Memories® Paper Paint, Satin Decoupage Medium; Eagle® Golden Taklon Brush; Bemiss-Jason Spectra® Art Tissue and Poster Board; Fiskars® Scissors & Paper Edgers

Clay Pot Mosaic

project provided courtesy of
FamilyFun Magazine

Turn trash into treasures by making
decorative pots with odds and ends
you might normally throw away.

You will need:
Newspaper
Pieces of broken pottery, tiles,
    beads, marbles, beach glass,
    shells or charms
Ceramic tile grout (available at
    hardware and craft stores)
Plastic knife
Terra cotta flower pot
Sponge

NOTE: It is very important to read and follow all manufacturer's directions when using grout.

1. Cover your work area with newspaper.
Note: Before you start decorating your pot, have a parent or adult go through your collection of pottery pieces and discard any that have sharp edges.

2. Spread a heavy layer of tile grout onto the flowerpot with a plastic knife. Press your assortment of decorative pieces carefully into the wet grout.

3. Spread a little more grout between the pieces so that most of the broken edges are covered.

4. After the pot is dry, wipe off any grout film with a damp sponge.

Spread layer of grout onto the flowerpot.

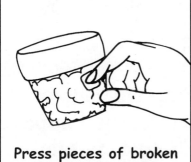

Press pieces of broken tile into the grout.

Spread grout between pieces to cover edges.

FamilyFun Magazine - 1(800)248-4849/www.familyfun.com

PUPPETRY

- Pop-Up Snake
- Craft Stick Puppets
- Jungle Scene
- Giant Stick Puppets
- Mini Marionette
- Stick Figures

Pop Up Snake

by Julie and Bill Stephani of Krause Publications

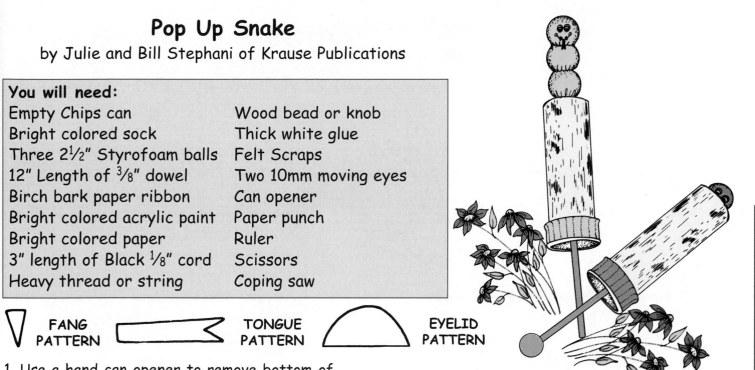

You will need:

Empty Chips can
Bright colored sock
Three 2½" Styrofoam balls
12" Length of ⅜" dowel
Birch bark paper ribbon
Bright colored acrylic paint
Bright colored paper
3" length of Black ⅛" cord
Heavy thread or string

Wood bead or knob
Thick white glue
Felt Scraps
Two 10mm moving eyes
Can opener
Paper punch
Ruler
Scissors
Coping saw

FANG PATTERN

TONGUE PATTERN

EYELID PATTERN

1. Use a hand can opener to remove bottom of can. Wrap strips of paper ribbon around can, overlapping slightly. (Can could also be covered with one 9" x 10" piece of paper of any color.) Cut ½" diameter circle in center of plastic lid. Set aside.

2. Paint dowel stick and knob if you wish.

3. Press a mouth indentation in one foam ball. Insert ball into toe of sock, checking mouth for correct position. Pull sock tightly around the ball then gather together at bottom of ball. Tie string tightly around gathers. Insert the second ball in the sock. Gather sock around the base then tie tightly with string. Apply glue to end of dowel and insert into third ball. Insert ball into sock then tie in same way at bottom of ball around dowel.

4. Cut the following from felt: 2 White fangs, 1 Red tongue, 2 Black eyelids and 2 (½ x 3")Black strips. Glue the eyes in place 1¼" apart then glue eyelids over eyes. Glue black cord along mouth indentation. Hold in place with straight pins until dry. Glue fangs and tongue in place as shown. Wrap felt strips around each joint, overlapping and gluing the ends in place. Use paper punch, to punch circles from several brightly colored papers. Glue these circles randomly around the snake.

5. Insert the snake into can. Fold ½" of sock cuff up and over the bottom of the can. Glue in place. Insert dowel into center of plastic lid. Press lid over end of can. Glue a wood knob or bead on the end of the dowel.

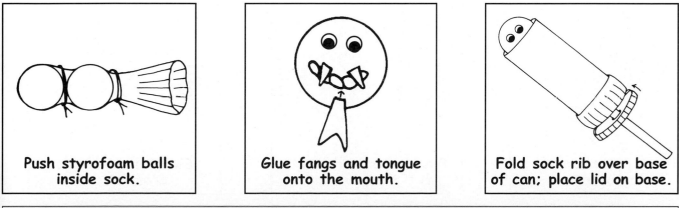

Push styrofoam balls inside sock.

Glue fangs and tongue onto the mouth.

Fold sock rib over base of can; place lid on base.

Dow Styrofoam® Brand Plastic Foam; Fiskars® School Scissors and Paper Edgers; Delta Ceramcoat® Acrylic Paint; Eagle Brush; Bemiss-Jason® Construction Paper; Darice® Craftwood Beads and Wiggle Eyes; Elmers® Craft Bond Tacky Glue

Jungle Stick Puppets

by Brenda L. Spitzer

Take a Safari and create your own characters right out of Africa. Visit the next pages to make the setting and animals.

You will need:
4 Craft sticks
One sheet each of Lime, Red, White, Turquoise, Purple, Gold, Beige, Pink and Gold Felt
Permanent black marker
3 Yellow 3mm pompoms
3 Green 3mm pompoms
4mm Wiggle eyes (2 per figure)
Scraps of Brown and Orange yarn
Gel glue
Ruler

1. Transfer patterns to felt. Cut out.

2. Glue heads, bodies or shirts and pants in place on craft stick.

3. For girl puppet, cut eight 3" lengths of brown yarn. Glue in place for hair. For boy, cut eight 1/2" lengths of orange yarn and glue in place for hair. Glue hats onto heads. Glue boots and hands in place. Glue on wiggle eyes. Use permanent markers to add details to faces and clothing. Glue pompoms in place for shirt buttons.

4. For cat, glue white oval to center of body. Glue arms, legs and tail in place on back of body. Glue red circles on paws. Glue purple collar at neck. Glue on wiggle eyes and a green 3mm pompom for nose. Add details with black marker.

5. For dog, glue arms, legs and tail in place on back of body. Glue ears in place on front of head. Glue on wiggle eyes and a green pompom for nose. Glue turquoise collar at neck. Glue pink circles on paws. Add details with black marker.

Trace pattern on to tag board.

Transfer patterns onto felt then cut out.

Glue felt pieces to craft stick.

Elmer's® Washable School Glue Gel; Fiskars® Ruler and Student Scissors; Dixon® RediSharp™ Marker; Forster® Craft Sticks; Darice® Felt Pompoms and Wiggle Eyes

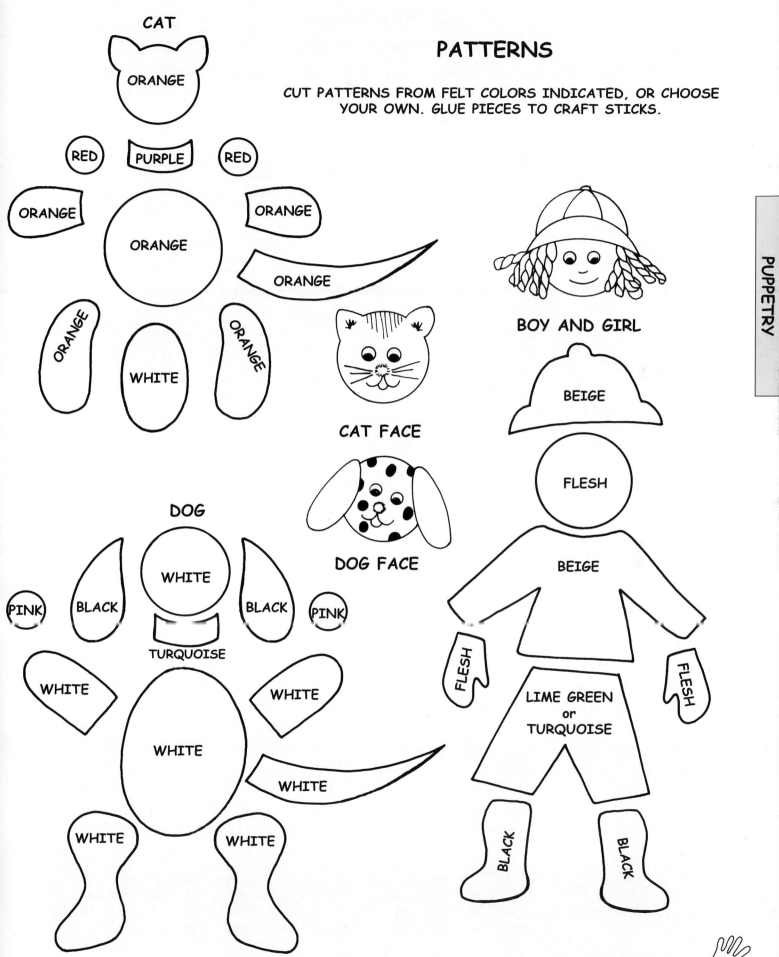

PATTERNS

CUT PATTERNS FROM FELT COLORS INDICATED, OR CHOOSE YOUR OWN. GLUE PIECES TO CRAFT STICKS.

CAT

ORANGE

RED PURPLE RED

ORANGE ORANGE ORANGE

ORANGE

ORANGE WHITE ORANGE

CAT FACE

BOY AND GIRL

BEIGE

FLESH

BEIGE

DOG

PINK BLACK WHITE BLACK PINK

TURQUOISE

WHITE WHITE

WHITE

WHITE WHITE

DOG FACE

FLESH FLESH

LIME GREEN or TURQUOISE

BLACK BLACK

Jungle Scene
by Brenda L. Spitzer

Create an entire jungle scene complete with animals, trees, and surprises. This is a perfect group project with each person contributing one part of the scene.

Jungle Base - You will need:
12" x 18" x 2" Styrofoam
Matte découpage medium
2" Sponge brush
Tissue paper - Yellow, Brown,
 shades of Green and Blue
Plastic Spoon
Decorative Glue

Use spoon to scoop out area for lake.

1. Run plastic spoon over candle wax then use spoon to carve out lake area and to round edges on the styrofoam sheet.

2. Use sponge brush to spread decoupage finish on lake. Overlap small torn pieces of tissue in various shades of blue on lake area.

3. Glue brown tissue pieces around outside edge of lake for land. Spread decoupage finish on a small section of land and overlap torn tissue pieces in various shades of green, yellow and brown. Repeat process until base is covered with tissue. Lightly coat base with decoupage finish. Let dry.

4. Brush decorative crystal glue over lake.

5. Use a pencil or skewer to make holes in the base to insert trees, grass, bushes, etc.

Elmer's® Craft Bond™ Decoupage Medium, School Glue Gel, Glow Creations™; Fiskars® Scissors, Craft Snips, Ruler; Dow Styrofoam® Brand Plastic Foam; Bemiss-Jason® Spectra™ Tissue Paper; Prang® Modeling Clay; Forster® Craft Sticks; Darice® Chenille Stems, Pompoms and Wiggle Eyes

Turtle - You will need:
1" Ball of Green modeling clay
½" Ball of Brown modeling clay
Two 3mm Wiggle eyes

1. Roll green clay into a 1" oval body. Flatten the bottom.
2. Add brown clay legs, a tail and head. Press wiggle eyes in place.
3. Seal with glue.

Snake - You will need:
3mm Tan chenille stem
3mm Black chenille stem
Two 3mm Wiggle eyes
Piece of Orange yarn

Twist tan and black chenille stems together. Cut to desired length. Glue wiggle eyes and a bit of orange yarn for tongue to one end.

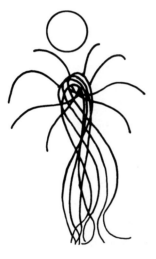

Palm Tree - You will need:
25 Tan 3mm chenille stems
3 Green bumpy 15mm chenille stems
Three ½" Tan pompoms

1. Bend a package of 25 tan chenille stems in half. Cut three green bumpy chenille stems in half. Place all green stems under the fold in tan stems and bend upward. Twist the tan stems together tightly.
2. Bend bottom ends of tan stems out about 1". Apply glue to end of each tan stem and insert in base.
3. Glue tan pompoms to center.

Monkey - You will need:
15mm Brown chenille stem
15 mm Brown bumpy chenille stem
½ " Tan pompom
Two 3mm Wiggle eyes

1. Wrap one end of a 15 mm brown chenille stem twice around a tan pompom for head. Fold remaining stem in half twice to form body. Twist stem at neck.
2. Cut a 15mm brown bumpy chenille stem into four sections for arms and legs. Bend ends of stems around body to attach. Glue wiggle eyes in place.

NOTE: When making chenille projects, twist chenille stems together as shown in the project diagrams. Your finished projects will look soft and furry when finished.

Bird - You will need:
6mm Irridescent chenille stems -
   White, Red or Green
3mm Tan chenille stem
3mm Yellow pompom
Two 3mm wiggle eyes

1. Cut a 4" length of irridescent tinsel stem. Bend in half and twist. Bend one end up slightly for the tail. Curve the other end up for neck.
2. Cut a 2" length of tan chenille stem. Twist it around center of bird and bend down for legs.
3. Glue on wiggle eyes and a 3mm yellow pompom for beak.

Bromeliads - You will need:
6 Green 6mm chenille stems
2 Tan 6mm chenille stems
6mm Green tinsel chenille stem
4 Green 15mm bumpy chenille stems
6mm Green or Gold tinsel stem
3 Red 7mm tinsel pompoms

1. Bend seven 6mm green and tan stems in half. Curve top of each stem downward. Cut one tinsel stem in half and curve top two ends into a spiral.
2. Place the bottom ends of all stems together with tinsel in the center and twist tightly. Use a pencil to make a small hole in the base. Apply glue to twisted ends and insert in hole.
3. Glue three 7mm tinsel pompom to the center of plant.

Alligator - You will need:
1" ball of modeling clay in Green
   and Black
Two 3mm wiggle eyes

1. Roll a 4" log of blended green and black clay. Taper the end of the log for the body. Roll four 1" long legs and attach to sides of body.
2. Draw scales on the alligator with a toothpick. Press on wiggle eyes.
3. Seal by painting surface with glue.

Rocks - You will need:
3/4" to 1 1/2" Styrofoam balls
1" Balls of modeling clay - Brown,
   White and Black

1. Run a plastic knife over candle wax then use to cut the bottoms from styrofoam balls. Cut balls into random shapes.
2. Mix balls of brown, black and white clay in the palm of your hand. Flatten the clay and wrap around styrofoam shapes.
3. Dip both ends of a toothpick in glue. Insert one end in the bottom of the rock and the other in the base. Brush glue over surface of the rocks to seal.

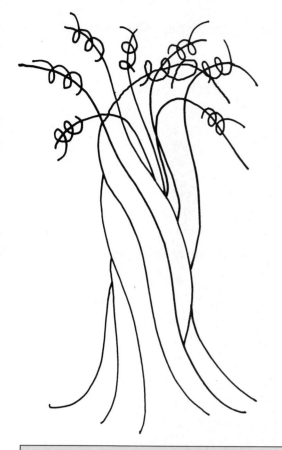

Frog & Lily Pad - You will need:
1" ball of modeling clay in Green
   and White
Two 3mm wiggle eyes

Leafy Tree - You will need:
15 mm Bumpy chenille stems -
   2 Black and 7 Brown
9 Brown 15mm chenille stems
18 Green 6mm chenille stems

1. Twist 7 brown and 2 black bumpy chenille stems together in the center. Bend out bottom bumps for tree roots. Bend top bumps out for branches.
2. To make longer branches, attach lengths of 15mm brown stems to the top bumps. Use 6mm green stems to make leaves. Twist the green stem around the base of a branch. Make a loop with the green stem and twist it. Wind green stem around branch and continue making loops to end of branch, adding green stems as needed.
3. Apply glue to bottom bumps and insert ends into bases. Make smaller shrubs the same way by using shorter lengths of chenille stems.

1. Roll a 1/2" ball with blended green and white clay for frog body. Make a 1/4" ball and attach for head. Use 1/4" balls for head and arms. Press two wiggle eyes in place. Add details with a toothpick.
2. Flatten a 3/4" ball for lily pad.
3. Glue frog and lily pad to base. Seal clay with glue.

Optional: Create grass from a variety of grass colored chenille stems. Vines can also be made by wrapping narrow stems around tree trunks and dangling them from branches. Make a sign post by wrapping brown chenille around one or two craft sticks then twist ends of stems together to make the post.

Creative possibilities are endless. See how many new ideas you and your friends can come up with!

Giant Stick Puppets

by Kathleen George

Gather up all sorts of odds and ends and your creativity to make giant puppets - on a stick of course! They might even look like you!

You will need (each puppet):
6" Styrofoam ball
7/16" dowel about 30" long
Glue
1" Paint brushes
Wood skewers
Scissors
Stapler
Curly chenille, yarn or tissue paper for hair
28 mm Wiggle eyes and eyelashes
Pompoms or beads
Assorted decorating material: Felt, foam, paper, ribbons, chenille stems

1. Paint both the styrofoam ball and stick with acrylic paint. Let dry. Push a skewer or pencil into the ball to make a handle while you paint. Push the handle into a big block of styrofoam while the paint dries. While you are working on the puppet, place the ball on a wide mouth jar to hold it steady.

2. Tips for Decorating: Attach objects to the ball with chenille stems, pipe cleaners, toothpicks or straws. Materials like yarn or cloth can also be pushed into the styrofoam with a tool such as a wooden skewer or pencil. First place a dot of white glue on the surface of the ball and push a bit of the material into the foam through the glue with your tool. When using delicate materials like tissue paper, fold a square of material in half, then in half again. Push the folded point into the foam with the blunt end of a skewer. Open the corners of the tissue when the glue is dry. When you want a stiff material to stick out straight from the ball (like a beak, nose or ears), make a slit in the foam first with a utility knife or sharp pencil. Squeeze glue into the slit before pushing the piece in place.

3. **Yarn Hair**: Wrap yarn around your hand or a piece of cardboard several times. Remove the loops from your hand and cut them open. Squeeze a line of glue where you would like a part in the hair. Push the ends of the yarn into the line of glue. After all the hair is attached and the glue is dry, you can give your puppet a hair cut!

4. **Eyes**: Shy or sleepy eyes are made by gluing a half circle of fabric over the top of a wiggly eye so that the pupil is slightly covered. Making eyelashes that point down emphasizes the look. To make eyes that look surprised, place the eyelashes at the top of the wiggly eyes pointing up. A bright colored eyelid glued on behind the lashes makes them stand out even more.

5. **Muzzle or Beak**: A muzzle or beak that flaps open needs to be made from a stiff material like foam. Fold over a rectangle of foam and staple firmly at the fold. Trim the front of the mouth as you please. You will need to make a deep slit in the styrofoam ball so that it sticks out without falling off the ball.

6. When you are finished, push the end of the dowel into the bottom of the ball about 3" deep, remove the stick, squeeze white glue into the hole and replace the stick. Decorate the stick if desired.

Dow Styrofoam® Brand Plastic Foam; Darice® Pompoms, Foamies™, Felt, Chenille, Wiggle Eyes; Bemiss-Jason® Construction Paper, Spectra™ Tissue Paper; Elmer's® Tacky Glue; Fiskars® Scissors and Paper Edgers; Forster® Skewers, Wood Dowels

Mini Marionette

by Patty Cox

You will need:
- 4 Red spaghetti oval beads
- 4 Black spaghetti oval beads
- 2 Red pony beads
- 3 Black pony beads
- Two 8mm wood beads
- 10mm Wood bead
- 10 "E" beads
- 2 Craft Sticks
- Quilting thread
- Needle
- ½" Hair-colored pompom
- Glue
- Red and Black fine tip markers
- Hand Drill

PUPPETRY

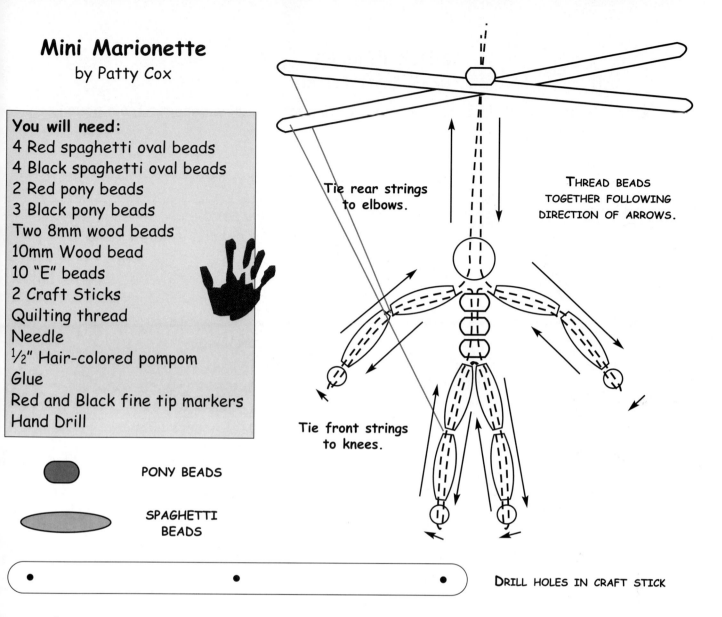

PONY BEADS

SPAGHETTI BEADS

Tie rear strings to elbows.

THREAD BEADS TOGETHER FOLLOWING DIRECTION OF ARROWS.

Tie front strings to knees.

DRILL HOLES IN CRAFT STICK

1. Drill $^1/_{16}$" holes in the center and ends of two craft sticks.

2. Thread beads together as follows: Thread a needle with 36" of quilting thread or embroidery floss. Bring needle down through top of head (10mm bead), through arm (2 red spaghetti beads) and hand (8mm bead). Loop thread round hand bead and return needle back through arm. Thread needle down through 2 red and a black pony bead. Thread needle through leg (two black spaghetti beads) and foot (black pony bead). Loop thread around foot then return needle through leg beads. Make second leg the same way. Bring needle back through body beads. Make second arm then return the needle through head bead.

3. Run thread through center holes of both craft sticks. Thread on a bead. Insert one thread end through the bead in one direction and the other in the opposite direction. Knot the ends of the thread together.

4. Tie 12" pieces of thread around each knee and elbow. Thread the opposite ends through holes in craft sticks as shown. Thread through E-beads on each side of craft stick then knot threads.

5. Glue on pompom hair. Draw eyes and smile on face using fine tip markers.

Darice® Spaghetti, Pony,"E", and Wood Beads, Pompoms; Dixon Redisharp™ Permanent Markers; Forster® Craft Sticks; Fiskars® Hand Drill; Elmer's® White School Glue

Stick Figures
by Lynda Scott Musante

You all know how to draw stick figures, now try creating stick figure puppets from pencils.

You will need:
Colored pencils
Tacky Glue
Scissors
2 Wiggle eyes per figure
5mm White pompoms
Mini candle cups
Yellow acrylic paint
1" Foam brush
Assorted Colored foam
Assorted Chenille stems
Assorted Feathers

1. Paint the candle cups yellow.

2. Glue on two eyes and a pompom nose. Dip feathers or pipe cleaners in glue and insert into the hole at the top.

3. Cut out two hand and two foot shapes from foam. Cut chenille stem in half. Glue hands on each end of one stem and feet on the ends of the other stem. Let dry.

4. Glue the candle cup to the eraser end of a pencil.

5. Tightly wrap center of hand stem around pencil so hands extend out to sides. Repeat with the feet. Bend chenille stems at the elbows and knees. Glue stems in place on the pencil.

Option: Cut foam pants, glue shoes to pants and then glue pants to pencil.

PATTERNS

Hands

Feet

Pants

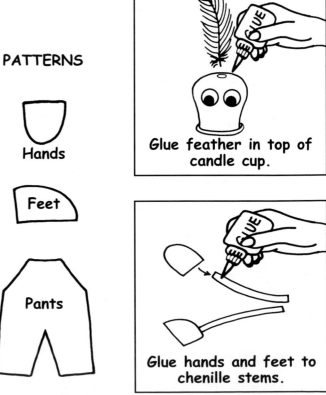

Glue feather in top of candle cup.

Glue hands and feet to chenille stems.

'TIS BETTER TO GIVE

- Desk Set
- Pony Bead Key Chain
- Etched Chore Jar
- Nesting Gift Boxes
- Sticks and ?
- Wrap It Up

Desk Set
by Brenda L. Spitzer

Make all four parts of this desk set by yourself, or find three friends and have fun making it together!

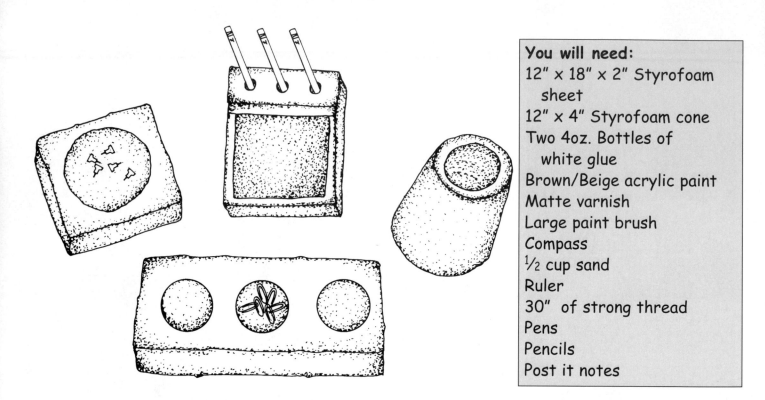

You will need:
12" x 18" x 2" Styrofoam sheet
12" x 4" Styrofoam cone
Two 4oz. Bottles of white glue
Brown/Beige acrylic paint
Matte varnish
Large paint brush
Compass
½ cup sand
Ruler
30" of strong thread
Pens
Pencils
Post it notes

1. Mark the styrofoam sheet into the following size sections: 4" x 4"; 4" x 5" and 4" x 9". Mark a line 6" from top of cone.

2. Wrap strong thread around both of your hands. Pull the thread tight and use it to cut through the marked sections on the styrofoam sheet. Run a plastic knife over candle wax. Use the knife to evenly trim all the edges. Use the knife to slightly angle the post-it note area downward on the 4" x 5" section. Center a pad of post-it notes on this area ³/₈" from bottom. Trace around it with a pencil. Use the knife to dig out an area ½" deep for the post-it notes. Make holes for pens and pencils by inserting them in the top of the sheet at an angle.

3. Use a safety compass and pencil to mark a 3" diameter circle in the center of the 4" x 4" sheet. Mark three 2¼" circles on the 4" x 9" sheet. Use a spoon to scoop out the circles to a depth of 1".

4. Cut the marked section off the top of the cone. Scoop out the center of the cone with a knife and spoon. Use a stiff brush to remove crumbs from all the pieces.

5. Mix glue with sand and paint in a plastic cup. Use a brush to apply this mixture to all top and inner surfaces. Allow to dry, then apply to all bottom surfaces.

6. When dry, apply matte varnish to seal.

Elmer's® School Glue Gel; Delta Ceramcoat® Acrylic Paint and Matte Varnish; Fiskars® Creative Works® Safety Compass; Dow Styrofoam® Brand Plastic Foam; Eagle Paint Brush

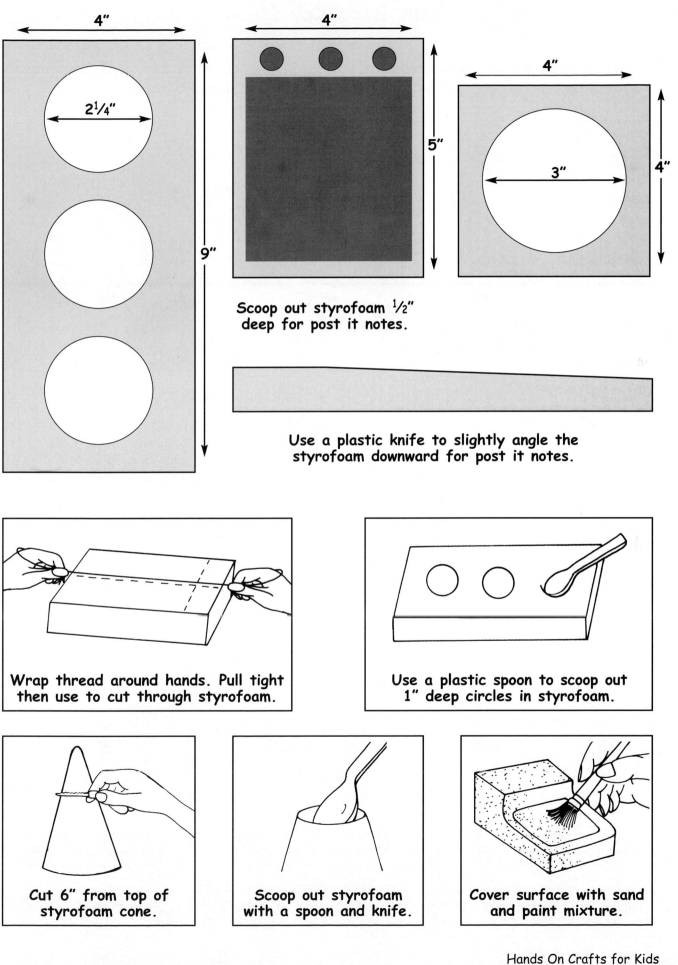

4"

2¼"

9"

4"

5"

Scoop out styrofoam ½"
deep for post it notes.

4"

3"

4"

Use a plastic knife to slightly angle the
styrofoam downward for post it notes.

Wrap thread around hands. Pull tight
then use to cut through styrofoam.

Use a plastic spoon to scoop out
1" deep circles in styrofoam.

Cut 6" from top of
styrofoam cone.

Scoop out styrofoam
with a spoon and knife.

Cover surface with sand
and paint mixture.

Pony Bead Key Chain
by Lynda Scott Musante

Once you've made one of these keychains, you'll want to make more for all of your friends. We show a baseball, but you can also make soccer balls, footballs, and more!

You will need:
2" Styrofoam ball or egg
Split ring key chain
Paper clip
Tacky Glue
Plastic knife
Baseball:
  7mm Red and White
  pony beads
Football:
  7mm Orange and Black
  pony beads
Orange acrylic paint
Paintbrush

BASEBALL:

1. Attach split ring to paper clip. Dip paper clip into tacky glue and insert into styrofoam ball.

2. Draw "seam" line on styrofoam ball with a pencil. Spread glue on ball along seam line with the plastic knife. Firmly press red pony beads into glue.

3. Working in sections, spread glue liberally onto the ball. Press white pony beads into the glue. Let dry.

FOOTBALL:

1. Carefully roll and press down on the large end of egg until it becomes the same size as the small end. Attach split ring to paper clip. Dip paper clip into tacky glue and insert into one end of the styrofoam egg.

2. Draw "seam" line on egg with a pencil. Spread glue on egg along seam line with plastic knife. Firmly press black pony beads into glue.

3. Make a mixture of orange paint and white glue. Working in sections, spread glue on the egg then press orange pony beads into the glue. Let dry.

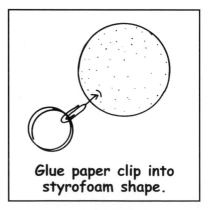

Glue paper clip into styrofoam shape.

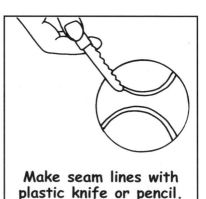

Make seam lines with plastic knife or pencil.

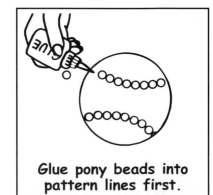

Glue pony beads into pattern lines first.

Darice® Pony Beads and Key Ring; Delta® Ceramcoat Acrylic Paint; Eagle® Golden Taklon Brushes; Dow Styrofoam® Brand Plastic Foam; Elmer's®Craftbond™ Tacky Glue

Etched Chore Jar

by Tracia Ledford Williams

Doing something nice for someone is the greatest gift of all. Fill this jar with cards listing chores or jobs you can do for a special person.

You will need:
Shimmery glass paint - White,
    Gold, Raspberry and Blue
White opaque glass paint
Surface conditioner and glaze
3" x 3" Compressed sponge
Black Permanent Marker
Scissors
3/4" Flat brush
Colored card stock
Decorative edge scissors

Sponge shapes onto surface of jar.

PATTERNS

Use a toothpick to make dot designs.

1. Brush surface conditioner over entire jar. Let the conditioner evaporate.
2. Sponge paint jar white. Let dry.
3. Trace star and heart shapes on compressed sponge. Cut out then rinse in water to expand. Wring out excess water.
4. Use glass paint to paint jar lid white. Let dry then apply a second coat.
5. Sponge raspberry hearts and gold stars onto the jar and lid.
6. Use a toothpick dipped in paint to make blue dots on jar and lid.
7. Apply an even coat of gloss glaze over the jar and lid. Let dry.
8. Add details around shapes and draw spirals with a black permanent marker.
9. Cut strips of colored paper with decorative scissors. Write on them different ways you can help around the house. Fold the strips in half and put them inside the jar. Here are a few suggestions:

Take out Trash
Bathe the Dog
Sweep the Floor
Fold Laundry

Delta® PermEnamels™ Glass Paint; Fiskars® Paper Edgers and Scissors; Bemiss-Jason® Railroad Board; Eagle® Golden Taklon Brushes

Nesting Boxes
by Mary Strouse from Year Round Fun
by Krause Publications

You will need:
2 Squares of paper per box
Glue
Pencil
Ruler
Scissors
Markers or crayons

NOTE: Each box should be made from a piece of paper 1" smaller than the previous one. Box lids should be ½" larger than the bottom of the box. For example; if a 5" square piece of paper is used for the box bottom, the lid should be made from a 5 ½" square. The next size box should be made from a 6" square of paper and the lid from a 6 ½" square.

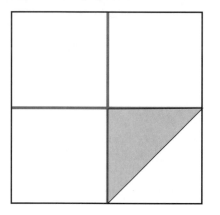

1. Mark center of square. Fold four outside corner points to center as shown.

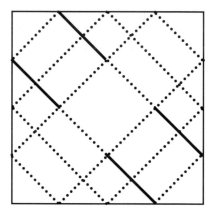

3. Unfold. Make four cuts. Do not cut into the center square.

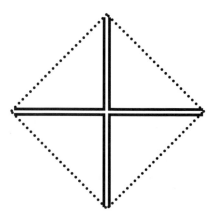

2. Fold one side, then the opposite side to the center. Unfold the two folded sides. Repeat with the other two sides.

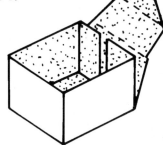

4. To assemble, refold the two largest corners (they look like big arrowheads). Fold ends in at a 90° angle so a box is formed. The last to be put into place are the two remaining corner points. Fold them up and over the sides to lock the box in place. Glue if desired. Decorate lids with paper shapes, or stickers.

Bemiss-Jason® Construction Paper;
Elmer's® White School Glue or Glue Stick; Fiskars® Scissors and Ruler

Sticks and ?

by Patty Cox

I bet you thought we were going to say "stones", but the next line is "clothespins". Here's a great gift to keep someone organized, or even yourself - a wall hanger for mittens, papers, or whatever you like.

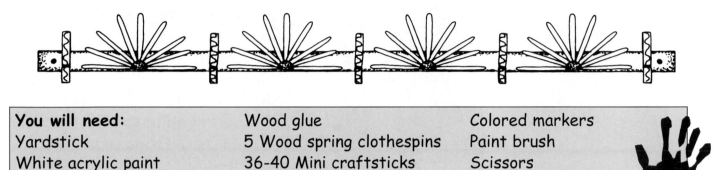

You will need:
Yardstick
White acrylic paint
Wood sealer

Wood glue
5 Wood spring clothespins
36-40 Mini craftsticks
4 Gold paillette sequins

Colored markers
Paint brush
Scissors
Hand drill

1. Drill $3/16"$ holes in yardstick, $3/4"$ from each end. Lightly sand yardstick and wipe away dust. Spray with a wood sealer.

2. Glue a clothespin $1^1/2"$ from each end and one at the 18" mark. Glue the remaining two clothespins between the others. Let dry.

3. Paint yardstick and clothespins white. Let dry.

4. Cut away the bottom third from four sequins. Center them between the clothespins, aligning bottom edges of sequins. Trace around each sequin for placement then glue five mini colored craft sticks just inside the pencil lines. Stack and glue the next layer of four on top. Glue the sequin on top of the craft sticks.

5. Draw squiggle lines on spring clothespins with colored markers or glue. Draw yellow dots between the squiggles.

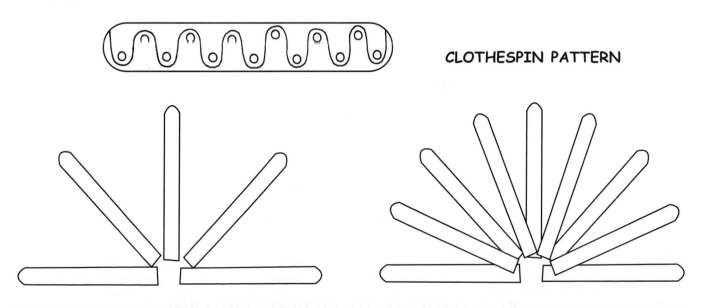

CLOTHESPIN PATTERN

Darice® Yardstick, Colored Mini Craft Sticks, and Sequins; Dixon® Markers; Delta® Wood Sealer and Ceramcoat® Acrylic Paint; Elmer's® Wood Glue, Squeeze Creations™; Fiskars® Hand Drill and Scissors; Forster® Spring Clothespins

'TIS BETTER TO GIVE

Hearty Friend
by Jennie McGuffee

A favorite early spring holiday is Valentine's day, but don't wait until then to make a very cute heart person for your favorite valentine. Ask your friends to make some too, then join them all together to make a valentine garland.

You will need:
2 Wood hearts
10 Mini spools
Red and Black Permanent Markers
Glitter Glue
Red metallic chenille stem
Tacky glue
Scissors
Wiggle eyes

1. Cut chenille stem in half. Twist the two halves together at the center.

2. Color hearts red with a marker. Draw a face on one heart with a black marker, or add glitter and wiggle eyes.

3. Glue the twisted chenille stems to the center of one heart at the back. Glue the second heart on top.

4. Thread two mini spools on two of the stems for arms and three spools on the other two stems for legs.

5. Wrap spools with ribbon, strips of fabric or chenille stems if desired.

6. Bend the ends of the chenille to hold the spools in place.

Darice® Wood Hearts, Wiggle Eyes, Chenille Stems and Mini Spools;
Elmer's® Tacky Glue, Squeeze Creations™ Glitter Glue; Fiskars® Scissors

Rocket Windsock

by Brenda L. Spitzer

Catch the wind with a windsock. Perfect for a breath of spring!

You will need:

12" x 18" White foam sheet	Red and Blue colored glue
9" x 12" Red foam sheet	Tacky glue
Two small Styrofoam wreaths - 3½" x ¾"	Scissors
	Paper Punch
Permanent markers - Red and Blue	Compass
	Ruler
3 Red, White and Blue plastic garbage bags	Kite string
	Tape

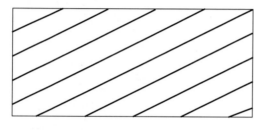

Draw diagonal stripes on foam.

STAR PATTERN

Knot ends of garbage strips on inside of foam.

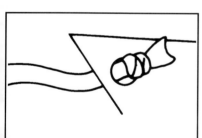

Glue foam around the styrofoam wreaths.

1. Draw diagonal pencil lines on white foam sheet as shown in diagram. Draw stars between the lines with red and blue markers. Go over pencil lines with red and blue glue. Let dry.

2. Punch holes 1" apart along the bottom edge of white foam sheet. Cut garbage bags lengthwise into 1" strips. Insert one end of each strip from front to back through the punched holes. Knot the ends on back of foam.

3. Apply tacky glue to one long edge on back of foam sheet. Apply glue around the outside of each styrofoam wreath. Bend wrong side of foam sheet around wreaths to form a cylinder. Overlap long edges. Hold in place with paper clips and tape until dry.

4. Use compass to make an 8½" circle on red foam. Cut out the circle and mark the center. Cut a wedge out of one side of the circle extending to the center. Cut a piece of kite string 36" long. Fold it in half and knot ends. Thread folded end through center of circle. Glue knotted end to inside of circle. Apply glue to one side of wedge cut. Bend around until edges overlap forming a cone. Allow to dry.

5. Cut four 1" x 4" strips of red foam. Glue one end of each strip to the top inside of cone. Let dry. Apply glue to outside of strips. Attach cone by inserting strips inside of cylinder. Let dry.

Darice® Foamies™; Fiskars® Safety Compass and Scissors; Elmer's® Craftbond™ Tacky Glue and Squeeze Creations™; Dow Styrofoam® Brand Plastic Foam

Spring Totem
by Lynda Scott Musante

Totems often feature wild creatures. Celebrate spring with a totem of bunnies, chicks and eggs. Each person can make one animal and then you can join them together to make a totem as tall as you'd like.

You will need:
3" x 4" x 1" Styrofoam block
Three 2½" Styrofoam eggs
Long skewers, or dowels
Tacky glue
Construction paper - Orange, Yellow and Pink
Acrylic paint - Yellow, Blue, Magenta and Gold glitter
Assorted Small pony beads
White pompom
Pearl head pins
Flower-shaped, or circle punch
Chenille stem - White, Yellow and Pink
Wiggle eyes
Scissors
2 Yellow feathers
1" Flat, or foam brush
Oval wood shapes

BASE: Cut styrofoam into a square with a plastic knife rubbed with candle wax. Rub the cut edges of the styrofoam together to smooth them. Use a foam brush to paint the base with glitter paint. Let dry. Punch yellow and pink flowers from construction paper. To attach flowers, insert pearl pin into a pony bead and then through the center of yellow flower. Dip the pin into glue and insert it into the sides of base. Alternate pink and yellow flowers around base.

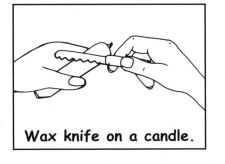

Wax knife on a candle.

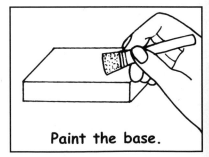

Paint the base.

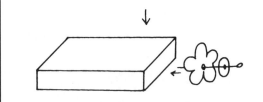

Thread a pony bead and punched paper flower onto a pin. Glue pin into sides of base.

EGGS: Hold eggs small end up and press on table to flatten bottom slightly. Push a craft stick through the center of each egg from top to bottom to make a handle. Paint each egg a different color then insert the craft stick into a scrap of styrofoam until the paint dries.

FLOWER EGG: Punch two yellow and two pink flowers from construction paper. Attach to egg with pin. Repeat with other flowers. Lightly crease and bend flower petals toward pin head for texture.

CHICK: Glue wiggle eyes on yellow egg. For beak, cut out a 1" square of orange construction paper. Fold the square diagonally and cut off the corners. Glue to egg under eyes. For wings, cut yellow chenille stem in half, bring the ends together and bend into a heart. Dip the cut ends in glue and insert them into the sides of egg. Fold wings back. For tail, cut two feathers 3" long. Dip the cut ends in glue and insert in back of egg.

BUNNY: Glue wiggle eyes to magenta egg. For ears, cut two 5" white and two 5" pink chenille stems. Fold one white and one pink stem in half with the white stem on the outside. Twist ends together then dip in glue and insert into the egg. Repeat for other ear. **Optional:** Paint oval wood shapes white, then glue in place for ears. For whiskers and nose, cut white chenille stem into four 2" pieces. Dip one end of stem into glue and insert under eyes. Repeat with the other three pieces to form an "X". Glue a small pompom at the intersection.

ASSEMBLE TOTEM POLE: Dip end of stick into glue and insert $1/2$" into center of base. Slide eggs onto skewer in the following order: Bunny, Flower Egg and Chick.

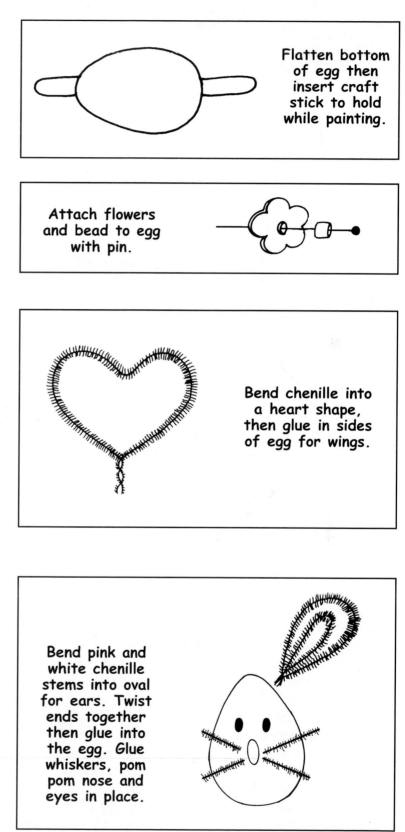

Flatten bottom of egg then insert craft stick to hold while painting.

Attach flowers and bead to egg with pin.

Bend chenille into a heart shape, then glue in sides of egg for wings.

Bend pink and white chenille stems into oval for ears. Twist ends together then glue into the egg. Glue whiskers, pom pom nose and eyes in place.

Dow Styrofoam® Brand Plastic Foam; Darice® Pony Beads, Chenille, Pompoms, Wiggle Eyes & Feathers; Elmer's® Craftbond™ Tacky Glue; Fiskars® Scissors & Punches; Bemiss-Jason Spectra® Construction Paper; Forster® Wood Skewers and Ovals; Eagle® Golden Taklon Brush

SPRING FORWARD

Eggs-citing
by Julie McGuffee for Craftworks Magazine

Make a basket of eggs and a bunny too, from Styrofoam and tissue paper.

You will need:
3" Styrofoam eggs
Two 2" Styrofoam eggs
Asstd. colors of non-bleeding tissue paper
White tissue paper
2 White bumpy chenille stems
Pink bumpy chenille stem
White foam
Tacky glue
Glitter glue
Paintbrush
6" of ¼" Ribbon
Paper clip
Scissors
½" Pink pompom for nose
Wiggle eyes

Mosaic Eggs

1. Choose 4-6 colors of tissue in pastel or bright colors. Tear three or four 1" wide strips from the end of the tissue sheets. Choose the lightest color and tear these strips into 1" pieces. Tear or cut the remaining strips into smaller pieces.

2. Push a pencil into the bottom of the egg to use for a handle. Squeeze tacky glue onto a paper plate. Wet the paintbrush with water and working with a small area at a time, spread glue over the surface of the egg. Place 1" squares of tissue on the egg, smoothing in place with the paintbrush and glue. Continue until the egg is completely covered with the lightest color.

3. Add smaller pieces of different colors of tissue on top of the base color, smoothing in place with the paintbrush and glue. Place randomly around the egg or arrange in a pattern.

4. Let dry. Re-coat the surface of the egg with glitter glue.

5. Unbend the paper clip to make a hook as shown. Push the narrow end into the top of the egg. Tie a bow around the top if desired.

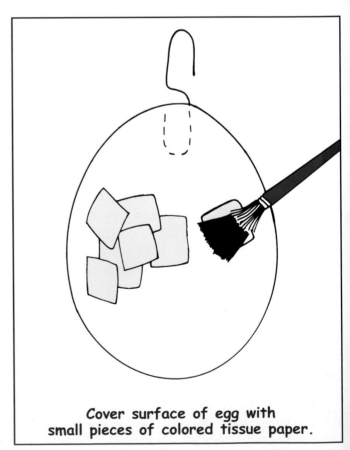

Cover surface of egg with small pieces of colored tissue paper.

EAR PATTERN

Rabbit

1. Cut two, 2" styrofoam eggs in half for feet and hands. Use a craft stick to make indentations on front of each piece for paws. Cover each piece and a 3" egg with small pieces of white tissue paper. Let the tissue paper dry.

2. Bend one white chenille stem in half. Twist at fold then push twisted end into base of egg. Push half a styrofoam egg onto opposite ends for feet. Cut a second chenille stem in half. Push one end into each side of the egg for arms. Glue remaining half eggs to opposite ends for paws.

3. Cut two ears from white foam. Glue a white (or pink) chenille "bump" to the center of each ear then glue the opposite end of the chenille into the head. Glue eyes and nose in place to finish.

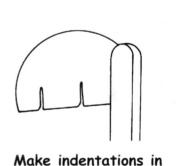

Make indentations in styrofoam for paws.

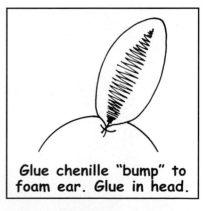

Glue chenille "bump" to foam ear. Glue in head.

Dow Styrofoam® Brand PlasticFoam; Darice® Foamies™ and Chenille; Elmer's® Craftbond™ Tacky Glue and Squeeze Creations™; Bemiss-Jason Spectra® Non Bleeding Tissue Paper

Metamorphosis of a Monarch Butterfly

by Sarah Stull

Follow the life cycle of a simply beautiful creature of the earth - the butterfly. You'll even learn some very interesting facts!

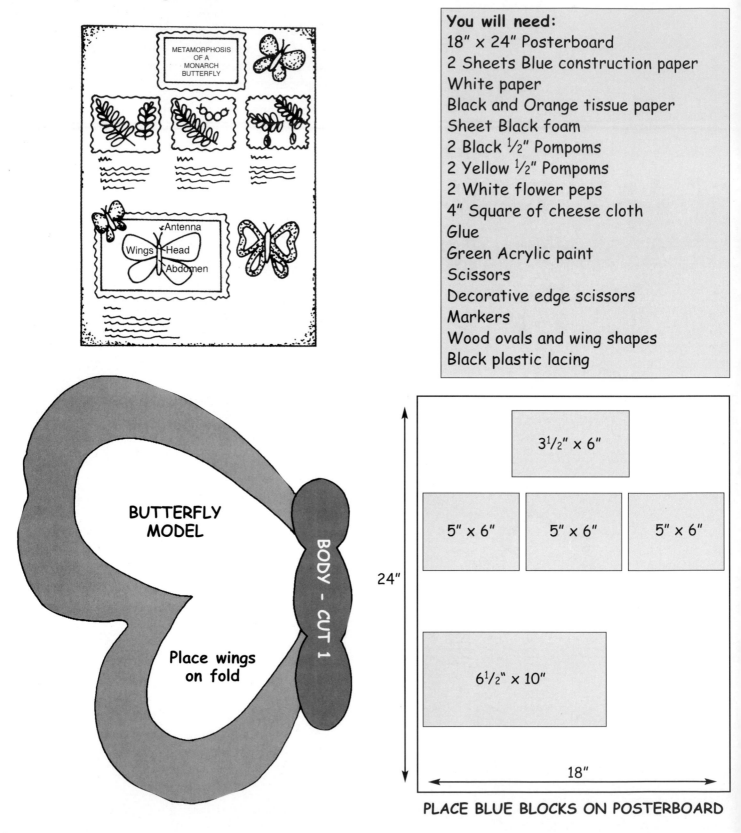

You will need:
18" x 24" Posterboard
2 Sheets Blue construction paper
White paper
Black and Orange tissue paper
Sheet Black foam
2 Black ½" Pompoms
2 Yellow ½" Pompoms
2 White flower peps
4" Square of cheese cloth
Glue
Green Acrylic paint
Scissors
Decorative edge scissors
Markers
Wood ovals and wing shapes
Black plastic lacing

BUTTERFLY MODEL

Place wings on fold

BODY - CUT 1

3½" x 6"

5" x 6"   5" x 6"   5" x 6"

24"

6½" x 10"

18"

PLACE BLUE BLOCKS ON POSTERBOARD

1. Cut the blue paper into 3½" x 6", 6½" x 10" and three 5" x 6" rectangles. Trim inside the cutting edge with decorative edge scissors.

2. Using diagram, lightly draw pencil lines for the placement of your blocks on the posterboard. Glue blue blocks in place.

3. Cut white paper into 3" x 5½" block and write **"Metamorphosis of a Monarch Butterfly"** with black marker. Glue on top of 3½" x 6" blue block.

4. **EGG:** Draw a multi-petaled leaf about 1" x 5" on white paper, draw little circles on each frond. Color leaf green and circles lighter green. Trim around shape. Take a real leaf from outside and lay it on wax paper. Coat with glue and let dry. Dab thick dots of glue on each frond for eggs. Let dry. Paint over dots with green paint. Glue picture and real leaf to first block.

5. **LARVA:** Draw a second leaf on white paper the same size as the first. Add a small caterpillar or larva. The larva should be no bigger than 1". Color larva black, yellow and leaf green. Trim around shape. Now glue pompoms together in chain alternating black and yellow. Cut each flower pep in half to make two antenna. Glue two on each end of the larva. Glue picture and larva model to second block.

6. **PUPA:** Draw an oval ½" x 2". Color it green. Trim then cut out. Crumple a scrap of paper. Cover with cheesecloth and shape into a 1" x 2" cocoon shape. Cover with glue and let dry and harden. Paint green. Use a needle and thread and sew through the top of the cocoon and tie off. This thread will be used to hang the pupa from a real leaf. Attach pupa picture and model to a board.

7. **ADULT:** Copy the diagram as shown on white paper. Outline with black marker and label all the parts. To make model, tape an 8" x 10" sheet of plastic wrap to a work surface. Cut black and orange tissue paper into 1" squares. Put some glue on the edge of the plastic. Dip brush in glue and then on a piece of tissue and place on plastic. Coat paper with glue. Keep adding squares of tissue alternating colors and gluing until you have an area about 7" x 7" covered with a mosaic of tissue paper. Coat the whole area again with glue. While it is drying, use the pattern and cut out the butterfly shape from black foam. Lay shape over center of tissue mosaic. Take lacing pieces and slide under body for legs (3 on each side) and under head for antenna. Use extra glue if needed. When dry trim around foam outline through all layers including plastic. Mount butterfly and drawing on board.

8. Color the oval and wing shaped wood pieces orange with markers or paint. Add Black lines and circles for wing patterns. Use to make butterflies to embellish your poster. Color a small wood teardrop shape black, then glue on top of the wings for the body.

9. On the empty white spaces label each section and include interesting facts about each stage of the metamorphosis. A few facts are given here but you'll have to research the rest.

EGGS: Are sticky so that they stay on the leaves even in wind. They hatch in 3 to 5 days.

LARVA: When larva are born they are only ⅛" long and 2" when fully grown. Larva have 8 pairs of legs. The larva gets its bad taste from the milkweed plant it eats.

PUPA: It takes 12 days for a butterfly to emerge from the pupa. The pupa hangs from the underside of a leaf.

ADULT: Monarchs are black, orange and white. The colors are made from small scales on the wings.

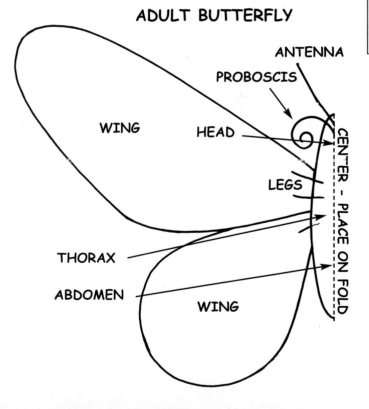

ADULT BUTTERFLY

SPRING FORWARD

Bird Bath
by Tracia Ledford Williams

Create a wonderful perch for your feathered friends from painted clay pots.

You will need:
Acrylic paint - Ivory, Spring Green, Green, Magenta, Black, Periwinkle Blue, and Yellow
Interior-exterior varnish
5" x 5" compressed sponge
Scissors
Pencil with new eraser
#5 Round brush
Small stencil brush
1" Sponge brush
Silicone Glue

1. Use the sponge brush to basecoat the bottom and sides of the saucer yellow, the bottom and sides of the pot blue and the top edge of the pot green.

2. Transfer the shapes to the compressed sponge and cut out. Dip the shapes in water to expand then wring out the excess.

3. Turn the flower pot upside down. Dip the flower petal sponge in ivory paint and make side view and full view daisies around the sides of the pot. Paint flower centers yellow then add ivory highlights and tiny black dots around the centers.

4. Dip leaf shapes in green paint and add leaves around the flowers. Use the round brush to paint stems and blades of grass.

5. Dip a pencil eraser in yellow and magenta and scatter dots around the pot.

6. Paint magenta ladybugs on flower stems and around the base of the pot. Using a round brush, paint the head, antennae, feet and body dots with black. Let dry.

7. Brush on 3 coats of matte varnish, allowing each coat to dry between applications.

8. Glue the saucer on top of the pot with silicone glue.
Note: Bring your birdbath indoors during freezing weather to prevent cracking.

PATTERNS

Large Leaf

Flower Petal

Ladybug

Small Leaf

Delta Ceramcoat® Acrylic Paint and Matte Interior-Exterior Varnish;
Eagle® Golden Taklon Brushes; Fiskars® Scissors

RAINY DAY FANTASY

- Dreams and Wishes Box
- Spiral Candles
- Disguise Yourself
- Checker Game
- Medieval Castle
- Who, What, Where and When

Dreams and Wishes Box
by Lynda Scott Musante

Gather up your dreams and wishes and collectibles to save them for a rainy day... or even a sunny one!

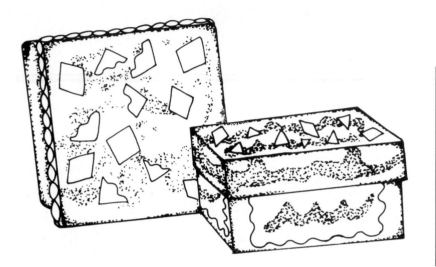

You will need:
Mini paper maché boxes
Decorative paper punches
Green acrylic paint
Flat brush
Decorative edge scissors
Scissors
Construction paper - asstd. colors
Decorative glue

1. Paint box and lid with acrylic paint. Let dry.

2. Punch out shapes from several colors of paper.

3. Squeeze out a squiggly line of decorative glue gel on lid. Place punched shapes onto glue. Squeeze out more glue gel to cover punched shapes.

4. Cut off edge of paper with decorative scissors. Turn the paper over and cut parallel to first cut, lining up pattern. Cut enough strips to go around the box lid.

5. Squeeze a thin line of glue gel along edge of box lid. Press strips into glue around box lid. Let dry.

Option: Cut small rectangles and glue to sides of box. Decorate with gel.

Squeeze a squiggly line of glue onto box top.

Press punched shapes into glue on lid.

Cover shapes with decorative glues.

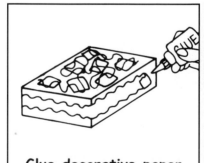

Glue decorative paper strip around lid.

Fiskars® Decorative Paper Punches, Paper Edgers, Student Scissors; Delta Ceramcoat® Acrylic Paint; Eagle® Golden Taklon Brush; Bemiss-Jason Rainbow® Construction Paper; Darice® Papier Mache; Elmer's® Squeeze Creations™

Spiral Candle

project provided courtesy of FamilyFun Magazine

This is a great project for groups. You can share scraps of colored wax to make lots of different combinations.

You will need:
Decorating wax strips
   (at least 2 colors)
Craft, or unserrated butter knife
Plain ball or short pillar candles

Lay the short piece of wax on top of the larger one.

1. Cut wax strips into two pieces - one 2³/₄" long and the other 2" long. Place the wax in warm, not hot water to soften.

2. Lay the shorter piece on top of the longer one then roll both pieces into a tight spiral log ¹/₂" in diameter and 1¹/₂" long.

3. When you've made about eight logs, use a knife to cut each one into as many slices as you can. Place wax slices in warm water to keep them soft and pliable.

4. Firmly press the wax slices all around the outside surface of the candle, starting at the base and working up. Continue placing the slices as closely together as possible until the whole surface of the candle is covered.

Roll the pieces of wax together.

Carefully slice the candle wax roll.

Press the slices onto the candle.

Disguise Yourself
by Patty Cox

Masks are the perfect prop for fantasy fun. Become whoever or whatever you'd like to be with just a few simple techniques.

You will need:

Foam Sheets - Red, Turquoise, Yellow and Fuschia	Rhinestones
	Glitter glue
	Elastic band
Assorted feathers	2 Pony beads
Masking tape	Scissors
Paillette sequins	Decorative scissors

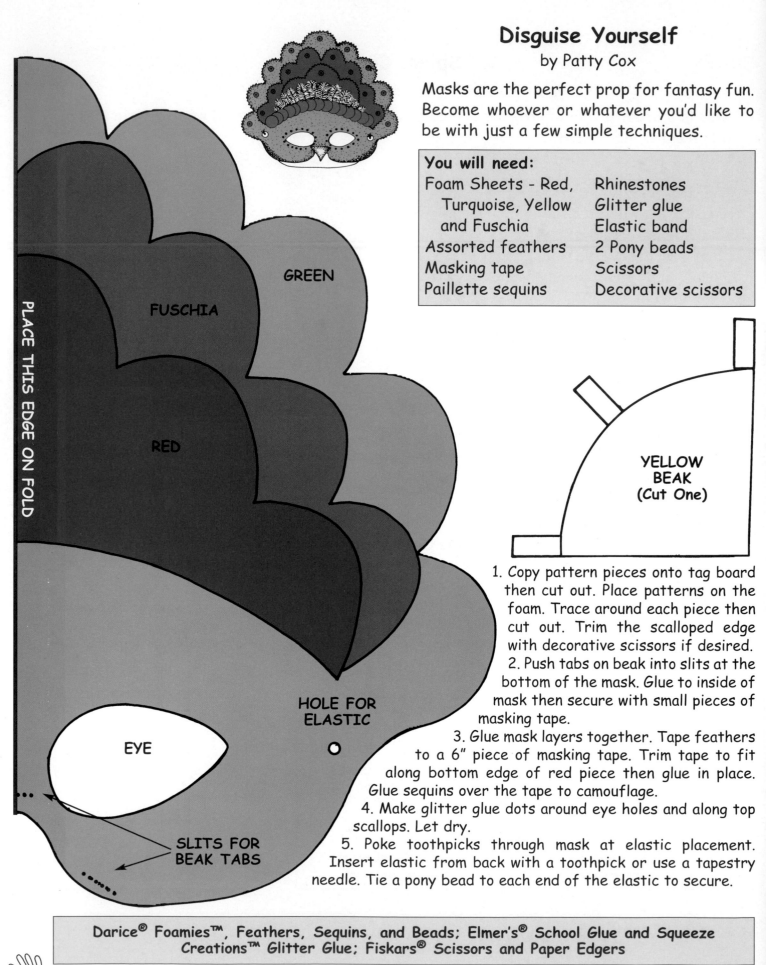

PLACE THIS EDGE ON FOLD

GREEN

FUSCHIA

RED

YELLOW BEAK (Cut One)

HOLE FOR ELASTIC

EYE

SLITS FOR BEAK TABS

1. Copy pattern pieces onto tag board then cut out. Place patterns on the foam. Trace around each piece then cut out. Trim the scalloped edge with decorative scissors if desired.

2. Push tabs on beak into slits at the bottom of the mask. Glue to inside of mask then secure with small pieces of masking tape.

3. Glue mask layers together. Tape feathers to a 6" piece of masking tape. Trim tape to fit along bottom edge of red piece then glue in place. Glue sequins over the tape to camouflage.

4. Make glitter glue dots around eye holes and along top scallops. Let dry.

5. Poke toothpicks through mask at elastic placement. Insert elastic from back with a toothpick or use a tapestry needle. Tie a pony bead to each end of the elastic to secure.

Darice® Foamies™, Feathers, Sequins, and Beads; Elmer's® School Glue and Squeeze Creations™ Glitter Glue; Fiskars® Scissors and Paper Edgers

Checkers Game
by Brenda L. Spitzer

Who says that checkers have to be black and red? Make your own game in a very creative way.

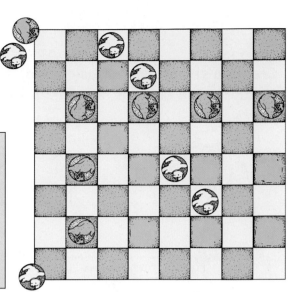

You will need:

3 Sheets of 22" x 28" White poster board	Dog and cat shaped sponges
1 Roll each of Yellow and Blue paper (min. 28" x 28")	Yellow acrylic paint
	Blue acrylic paint
Gel glue	Black permanent marker
24 Wood discs - 3"	#1 Round brush
	Scissors

1. Divide yellow and blue paper into eight strips, 3½" wide x 28" long.

2. Cut two, 6" x 28" strips of white poster board. Adding the additional strips to the 28" side of the the posterboard, glue two layers of posterboard together to make a square 28" x 28" as shown.

3. Place yellow paper strips across 28" square. Starting at the lower left side, glue end of every other yellow strip in place.

4. To weave the checkerboard pattern, place a blue paper strip horizontally at the bottom of the square. Glue left end of blue strip in place on top of the yellow strip on lower left corner. Weave blue strip under and over yellow strips at bottom of square, gluing lower edges in place as you weave. The next blue strip will begin under the yellow strip on the left side. Glue left end of blue strip in place.

Weave over and under the yellow strips gluing right end in place. Repeat with remaining blue strips to cover 28" square. Set aside to dry.

5. Paint twelve discs yellow and twelve discs blue. Set aside to dry.

6. Dip dog and cat sponges in water then wring out well. Spread some yellow paint on a paper plate. Dip dog sponge into paint. Work paint into sponge by lightly pressing sponge up and down on plate. Sponge paint dog shapes on one side of all blue discs. Use small paint brush to spread paint evenly on sponge painted image. Let dry. Next, sponge blue cats on the yellow discs. Let dry.

7. Outline dog and cat shapes and add details with black marker.

Option: For extra protection, apply a layer of clear, adhesive backed film to top of the board.

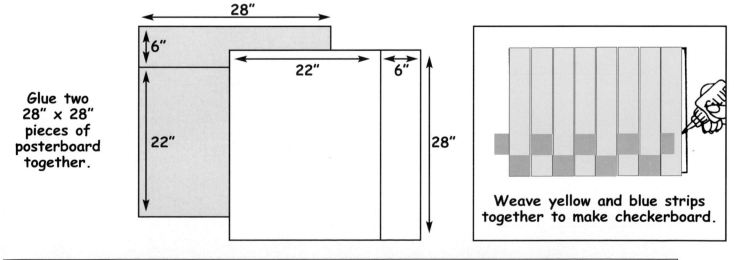

Glue two 28" x 28" pieces of posterboard together.

Weave yellow and blue strips together to make checkerboard.

Bemiss-Jason Poster Board, Fadeless™ Paper Rolls and (optional) Protecto Film®; Elmer's® Gel School glue; Delta Ceramcoat® Acrylic Paint; Fiskars® Shapes and Forms Sponges, Ruler and Scissors; Eagle® Golden Taklon Brush; Darice® Craftwood

Medieval Castle
by Kathleen George

Create a styrofoam fantasy world. Make a medieval castle complete with drawbridge, but you'll have to supply the dragons, knights in shining armor and damsels in distress from your imagination.

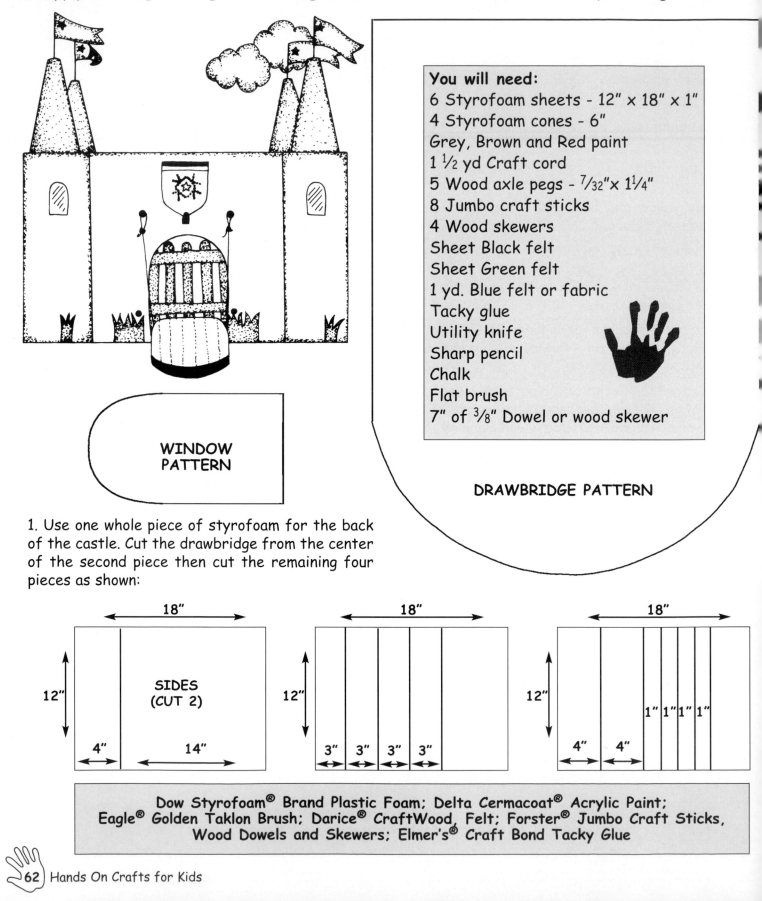

You will need:
6 Styrofoam sheets - 12" x 18" x 1"
4 Styrofoam cones - 6"
Grey, Brown and Red paint
1 ½ yd Craft cord
5 Wood axle pegs - $^{7}/_{32}$" x 1¼"
8 Jumbo craft sticks
4 Wood skewers
Sheet Black felt
Sheet Green felt
1 yd. Blue felt or fabric
Tacky glue
Utility knife
Sharp pencil
Chalk
Flat brush
7" of $^{3}/_{8}$" Dowel or wood skewer

WINDOW PATTERN

DRAWBRIDGE PATTERN

1. Use one whole piece of styrofoam for the back of the castle. Cut the drawbridge from the center of the second piece then cut the remaining four pieces as shown:

18"

12"

SIDES (CUT 2)

4"   14"

18"

12"

3" 3" 3" 3"

18"

12"

1" 1" 1" 1"

4"   4"

Dow Styrofoam® Brand Plastic Foam; Delta Cermacoat® Acrylic Paint; Eagle® Golden Taklon Brush; Darice® CraftWood, Felt; Forster® Jumbo Craft Sticks, Wood Dowels and Skewers; Elmer's® Craft Bond Tacky Glue

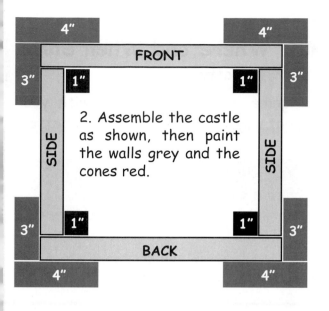

2. Assemble the castle as shown, then paint the walls grey and the cones red.

3. Use a craft stick to draw lines in the drawbridge for planks. Press a skewer into the styrofoam across the bottom of the drawbridge about ½" from the edge. Glue in place. Paint the drawbridge brown. Let dry.

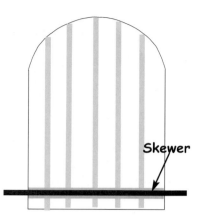

Skewer

4. Use a craft stick to make a 2" long channel on either side of the drawbridge opening, ½" from the bottom edge at the front of the castle. Put the drawbridge in place so that the ends of the skewers rest in these channels. Cut patches of grass from green felt, then glue to the castle front over the ends of the skewers to hold them in place.

Channels for ends of skewer.

Grass

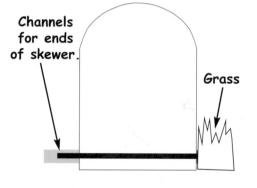

5. Push four axle pegs into the styrofoam, two on either side of the drawbridge as shown. Cut two lengths of cord that measure the distance from the top edge of the drawbridge when the bridge is open to the top peg plus 3 inches. Use a pencil to push one end of each cord into the top of the drawbridge. Glue in place. Make a loop at the opposite end of the cord. When the drawbridge is closed the cords will run over the top axle peg and the loop will hook over the lower axle peg. Lower the bridge by unhooking the loop.

Axle pegs and cord assembly.

6. Make a portcullis by gluing craft sticks together as shown. Tie two 12" lengths of cord to the top of the portcullis so it can be raised and lowered. Keep in place by making loops in the cord. These will hook over axle pegs and can be used to keep the portcullis open or closed. Hang the portcullis behind the drawbridge opening on the inside of the castle.

7. To make a catapult, glue a bottle cap to one end of a craft stick, then glue the craft stick across the side of a small spool.

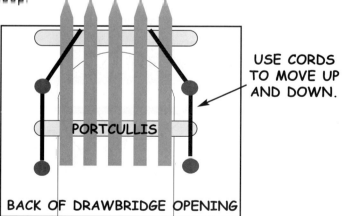

USE CORDS TO MOVE UP AND DOWN.

PORTCULLIS

BACK OF DRAWBRIDGE OPENING

8. Place the castle on a piece of blue felt for the moat, then cut windows from black felt. Banners and flags can also be cut from felt and used to decorate your castle. Embellish a banner with sequins then glue to the front of the castle over the drawbridge. Flags can be glue to skewers then pushed into the tops of the cones.

Memory Game
by Julie McGuffee

In this updated version of the matching game, use reprints of old photos to learn about your family.

1. Glue metallic paper to posterboard then cut into eighteen 3" x 4" pieces. Round the corners of the cards with corner scissors, or scissors.

2. Use the oval template, or an oval cutter to cut out photographs about 1" smaller than the size of the card. Glue photographs to the sheets of construction paper. Identical photographs should be glued to the same color sheet. Cut around the photograph about 1/4" from the edge with decorative scissors. Glue to the center of the white side of the cards.

3. Paint over the photograph side of the card with gloss decoupage sealer.

Rules of the Game: Mix the cards up and place them face down on a table or the floor. The first player turns over two cards. If the cards match, the player keeps them both and plays again. If they don't match the player turns the cards over and another player chooses two cards and tries to make a match. The player with the most pairs of cards is the winner!

Option: Make additional pairs of cards to make your game even more interesting. Pairs could be husband and wife, brother and sister, grandmother and grandfather, aunt and uncle, etc. You could even write the person's name on one card and have their photograph on the other.

Use an oval template to crop your photograph.

Glue photo to colored paper then trim with decorative scissors.

School Travels Scrapbook Page
by Jennie McGuffee

Choose your favorite design, a school bus or design your own fancy race car. Display your school pictures or pictures of friends in the windows, or around your page.

You will need:
8" x 10" Heavy White paper
Yellow embossed paper
Shiny Black corrugated paper
Red construction paper
Black and Red permanent markers
Silver metallic paper
½" Hole punch
Scissors
Corner scissors
Glue stick
Circle cutter or compass and scissors
Stickers

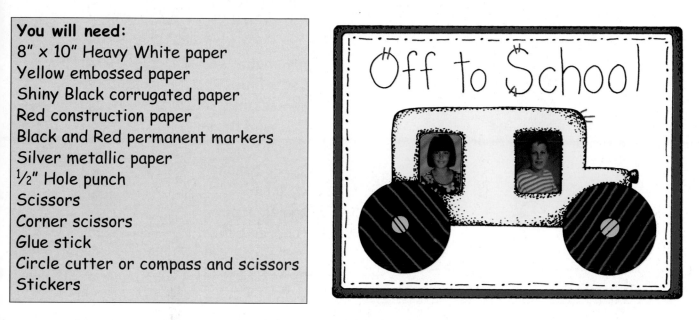

1. Cut a 6½" x 4" rectangle and a 1½" x 2" rectangle from waffle paper. Round upper corner of the rectangles. Cut two windows in the large rectangle large enough for your photographs.

2. Cut two black corrugated paper circles. **Note**: It is easier to draw patterns on and cut from the back of the corrugated paper. Glue the yellow rectangles in place on the white paper, then glue the black circle wheels in place. Punch two circles from silver metallic paper and glue them to center of the wheels.

3. Use the black and red markers to decorate the edge of the paper and to write a title on your page. Add stickers if desired. Glue the white paper to the center of the red construction paper.

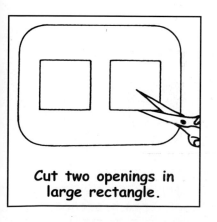

Cut two openings in large rectangle.

Glue rectangles to White paper.

Glue wheels in place then decorate.

Bemiss-Jason Spectra® Construction Paper, Metallic Corobuff™, Waffle™ Paper; Fiskars® Circle Cutter, Corner Edgers, Student, Stickers and Hole Punch; Elmer's® Gel Glue

Family Tree
by Tracia Ledford Williams

Making a family tree is a perfect family project for all ages.

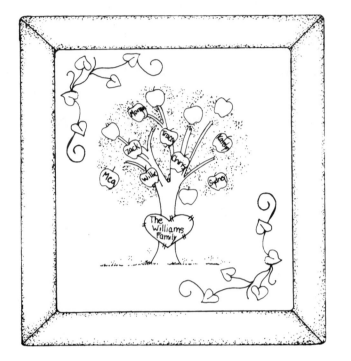

You will need:
White Card stock 11" x 14"
Frame and mat with 8" x 10" opening
Paper paint - Green, Sage Green,
  Brite Blue, Red, Chocolate Brown,
  White, and Yellow,
#5 Round brush
Stencil brush
Black permanent marker
Scissors
Tracing paper
Transfer paper
Small piece of compressed sponge
Tape

1. Transfer the patterns to card stock. Use the round brush to paint the trunk and branch chocolate brown.

2. Dip an old scruffy brush into sage green and tap the color on the tree for the leaves. Dip a corner of the brush into green and add some darker touches to add depth. Tap some grass around the bottom of the tree. Let dry.

3. Transfer the apple pattern to compressed sponge. Cut out the shape, dip in water to expand then wring out excess. Dip sponge into red paint then press the apple shapes on the tree.

4. Paint the heart shape yellow. Let dry.

5. Write your family name on the heart. Outline the apples, tree trunks and apple stems. Add names to apples.

6. Add tiny dot bright blue and yellow flowers around the base of the tree.

7. To make the design on the mat, transfer the leaf pattern to compressed sponge and dip in a mixture of one part green and one part sage green. Add tiny vines connecting the leaves using the tip of a round brush. Add yellow dots around the vines and leaves.

Paint the tree trunk Chocolate Brown.

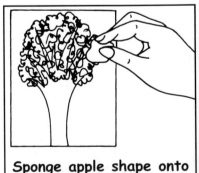

Sponge apple shape onto tree branches.

Delta® Cherished Memories™ Acid Free Paper Paint;
Bemiss-Jason Spectra® Railroad Board; Eagle® Golden Taklon Brush

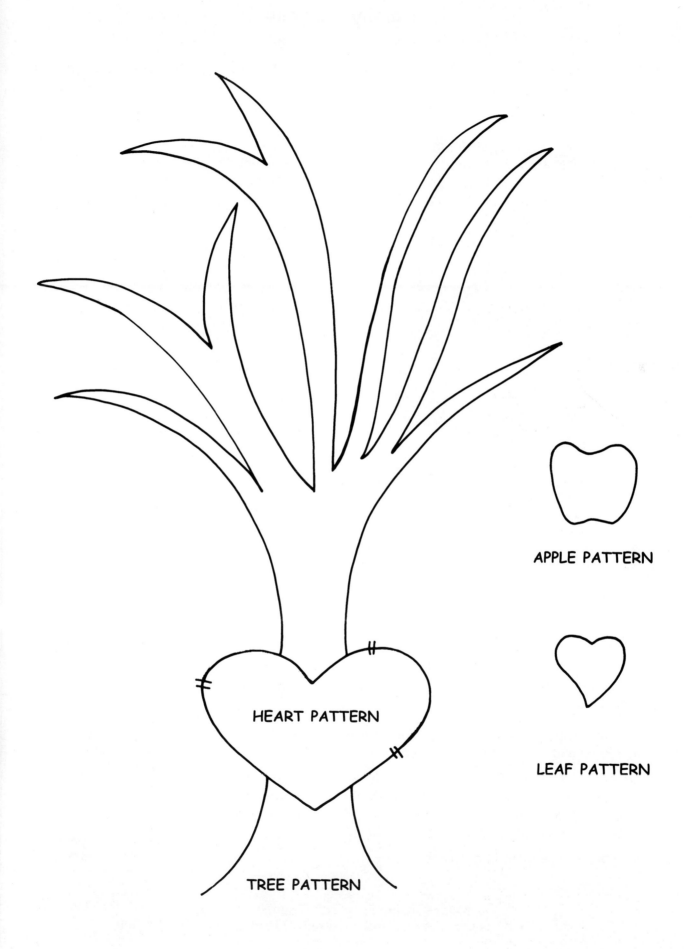

APPLE PATTERN

HEART PATTERN

LEAF PATTERN

TREE PATTERN

Family Recipes
by Carol Scheffler

Does your grandma bake special treats when you visit? How about traditional holiday meals that you look forward to each year? The recipes for these foods are important to you and your parents. Learn to make a scrapbook of these special family recipes.

You will need:
Black card stock 8½" x 11"
White card stock 5" x 7"
White sticker paper 8½" x 11"
M&M rubber stamp
Dye base ink pads - Red, Yellow, Green, Brown and blue
Decorative edge scissors
Scissors
Glue stick
Recipe and significant story printed by hand or computer on 4" x 6" Yellow paper

1. Tap the rubber side of the "M&M" stamp lightly several times on the yellow ink pad. Press the stamp on the white cardstock, taking care not to rock or wiggle the stamp. Lift the stamp straight off. Stamp the image again without re-inking. (You can print an image several times without having to re-ink.)

2. Continue stamping yellow "M&M"s randomly over the card. Don't stamp the center section.

3. Wash off the stamp and ink it on the red ink pad. Stamp the red "M&M"s randomly over the card.

4. Stamp "M&M"s in three other colors randomly all over the card.

5. Trim a favorite family recipe and a story about it with the fancy-edged scissors.

6. Glue the recipe to the center of the stamped card. Glue the stamped card and the story to the black cardstock.

7. Stamp four "M&M"s in various colors on the white sticker paper. Cut them out with scissors. Stick the "M&M"s to the lower right hand corner of the recipe card, overlapping them slightly. Stick one "M&M" to lower right corner of the story.

8. Place your recipe page in a scrapbook.

Stamp design around edge of card.

Glue to papers to Black cardstock.

Bemiss-Jason Spectra® Railroad board;
Fiskars® Paper Edgers and Scissors; Elmer's® Gel Glue Stick

Try some of our 'Hands On' recipes, then tell a story about how you made them!

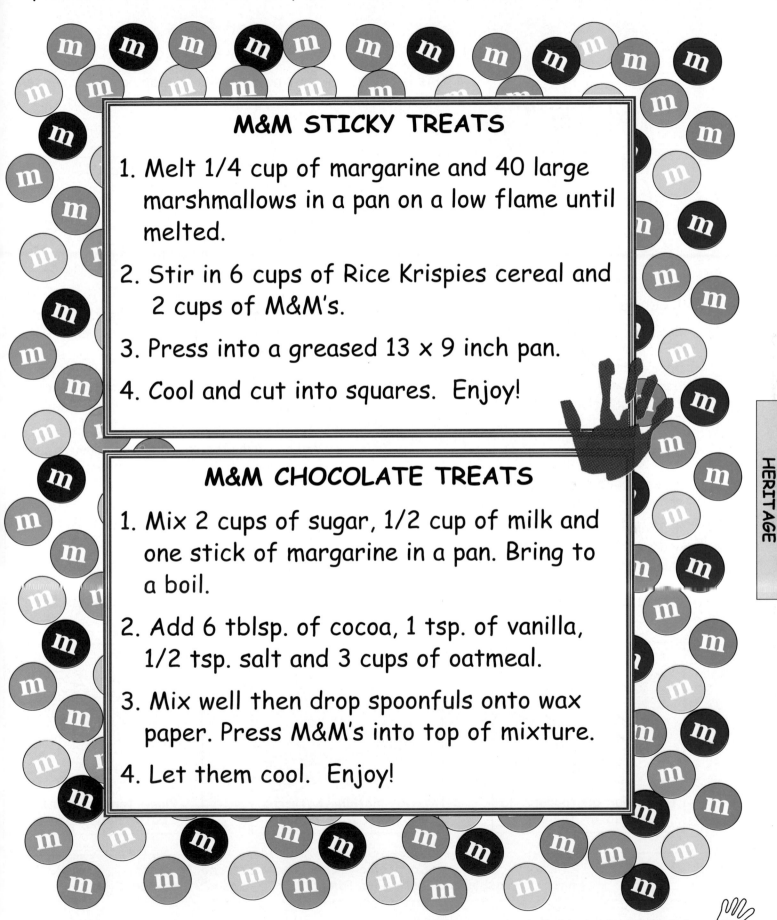

M&M STICKY TREATS

1. Melt 1/4 cup of margarine and 40 large marshmallows in a pan on a low flame until melted.

2. Stir in 6 cups of Rice Krispies cereal and 2 cups of M&M's.

3. Press into a greased 13 x 9 inch pan.

4. Cool and cut into squares. Enjoy!

M&M CHOCOLATE TREATS

1. Mix 2 cups of sugar, 1/2 cup of milk and one stick of margarine in a pan. Bring to a boil.

2. Add 6 tblsp. of cocoa, 1 tsp. of vanilla, 1/2 tsp. salt and 3 cups of oatmeal.

3. Mix well then drop spoonfuls onto wax paper. Press M&M's into top of mixture.

4. Let them cool. Enjoy!

Paper Dolls
by Cindy Gorder

This is one craft that never loses its popularity. Create a doll that looks just like you and reflects your heritage.

You will need:	Decorative papers
Small school photo	Scissors
White tag board	Glue Stick
Colored card stock in your skin tone	Pencil
	Black fine-tip marker

1. Cut the base from tagboard.

2. Cut bodies from card stock and glue to base. If you are cutting a boy, use the shoes on the base pattern. After you glue the body on the base, draw lines between the shoes and the legs for socks. Color the shoes black with a marker. If you are cutting a girl, don't include the shoes on the base pattern. Color the shoes on the girl body black.

3. Carefully cut your head and hair from a school picture and glue on the body.

4. Transfer the clothing patterns to card stock and cut them out. NOTE: You are going to keep the templates (rectangles of card stock with the openings) - not the middle pieces. Lay the templates on the papers of your choice and trace. If using a solid color flip the template over and draw on the back of the paper - then you won't have to erase pencil lines. If using patterned paper, the template allows you to place the design of the paper on the clothing most appropriately. Erase any pencil lines that remain after cutting out the garment.

5. You can alter the shape of the garment, using the template as a guide. For example you can make the skirt shorter and flared at the bottom. Make the sleeves on the T-shirt longer and wider or even make a V-neckline instead of a round one.

6. If you like, you can draw details on the clothing and decorate with other cut-out shapes and images, or even embellish them with stickers.

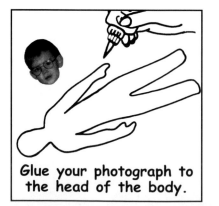

Glue your photograph to the head of the body.

Trace clothing patterns onto card then cut out.

Place template onto patterned paper.

Fiskars® Scissors, Card stock, Paper booklets and Stickers; Elmer's® Washable School Glue Stick; Bemiss-Jason® Tag Board.

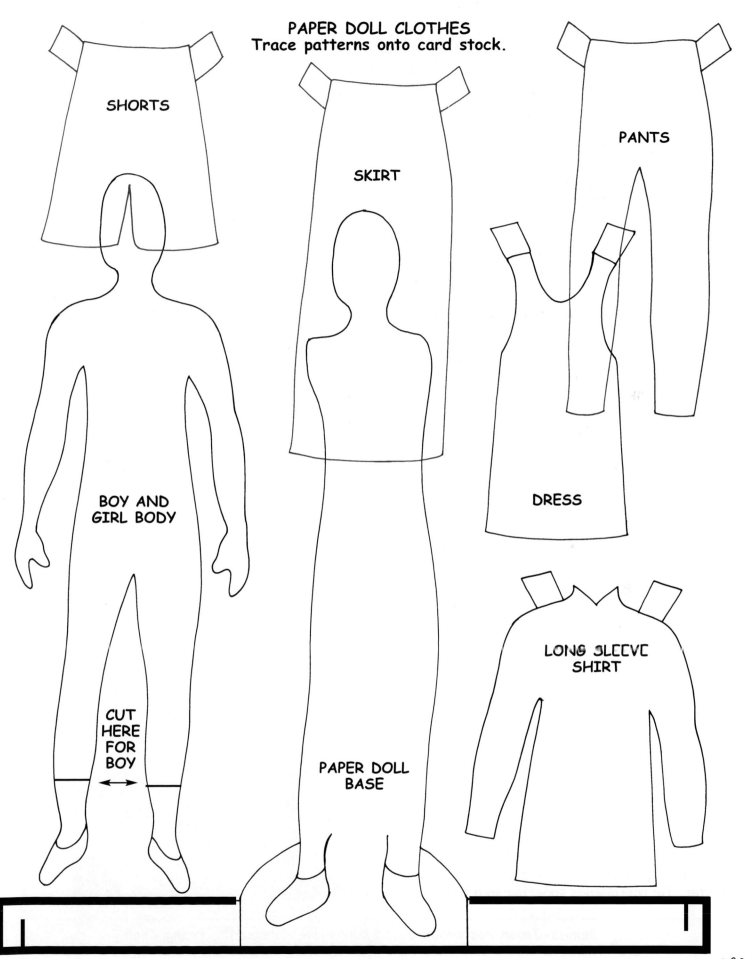

PAPER DOLL CLOTHES
Trace patterns onto card stock.

SHORTS

SKIRT

PANTS

BOY AND
GIRL BODY

DRESS

CUT
HERE
FOR
BOY

LONG SLEEVE
SHIRT

PAPER DOLL
BASE

Birthday Greetings
by Patty Cox

Never forget a friend's birthday again! Create this unique birthday wheel to remind yourself of those very important days of the year.

You will need:
Circle Cutter or compass and scissors
Construction Paper - 2 Light colors
  and assorted bright colors
Tie tack
Paper punches
Extra fine markers
Glue stick
Photo copies of friend's photos

1. Cut a 6½" and a 5¾" circle from construction paper using a circle cutter or scissors and a compass.

2. Cut windows out of the smaller circle using pattern given.

3. Lightly pencil the eight pie shaped wedges on the bottom circle.

4. Assemble circles with a tie tack. Turn wheel to each wedge. Trace inside photo window of each wedge for positioning.

5. Remove the tie tack. Glue a photo in each photo window on bottom wheel using a glue stick.

6. Punch heart and triangles from several colors of construction paper. Glue triangles on top wheel. Write "Phone" on punched shapes next to top window. Write "Birthday" next to smaller bottom window, then write "Friendly Facts" at the bottom of the wheel.

7. Assemble wheel with tie tack. Rotate wheel over a photo. Write the person's phone number above their photo and their birth date under their photo.

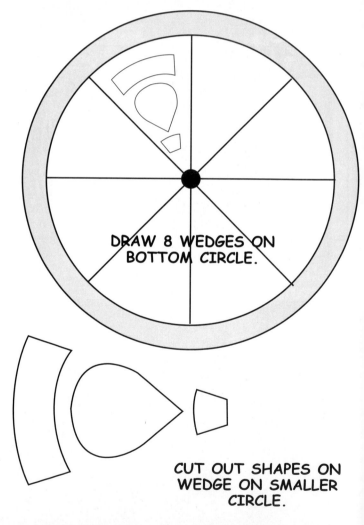

DRAW 8 WEDGES ON BOTTOM CIRCLE.

CUT OUT SHAPES ON WEDGE ON SMALLER CIRCLE.

Bemiss-Jason Spectra® Acid Free Construction Paper; Dixon Redisharp® Markers; Elmer's® Glue Stick; Fiskars® Compass, Scissors, Punches and Circle Cutter

Candy Party Favors

by Sandi Egan and Kay Zaia for Party Projects for Design Originals

Combine two of your favorite things, candy and parties for fun party favors.

You will need:
Assorted candy (kisses and rolls)
5mm Black pompoms
Tinsel chenille stems
Black construction paper
Wiggle eyes
2" Gold cord
1/4" White pompom
Metallic Cupcake or candy holders
Glue
Scissors

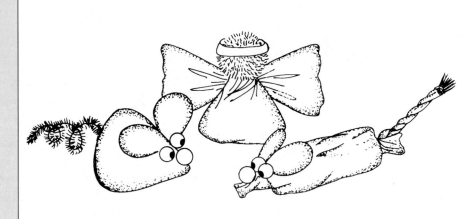

Angels

Wings: Cut bonbon cup in half.
Body: Glue 1/4" white pompom on top of gold kiss. Glue wings on back.
Halo: Cut 2 1/4" of gold cord, bend in circle and glue on back of pompom.

Candy Roll Mice

Twist ends of candy roll wrapper to a point.
Ears: Cut heart from black paper. Fold in half, open and cut down crease 1/4". Push heart open and glue on front of candy roll.
Face: Glue 6mm wiggle eyes and a 5mm black pompom on front of candy roll.
Tail: Glue 2" of yarn to back of candy roll.

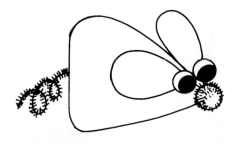

Candy Kiss Mice

Tail: With thumb and forefinger, wrap tinsel around once, make an S and curl up. Glue on bottom of kiss.
Ears: Cut mini heart from black paper. Fold in half, open and cut down crease 1/2". Push heart open and glue on front of mouse.
Eyes: Glue 6mm wiggle eyes on front.
Nose: Glue 5mm black pompom on tip.

Fiskars® Scissors; Darice® Metallic Chenille Stems, Pompoms and Wiggle Eyes; Elmer's® Craft Bond Tacky Glue

"Light" of the Party
by Julie McGuffee

Light up an outdoor party with colorful paper lanterns.

You will need:
14" x 12" sheet of two-tone paper
Decorative scissors
Star paper punch
Glue stick

Make straight, or diagonal cuts from fold up to the folded edge of paper.

1. Cut paper in half so that each piece measures 7" x 12". Turn the long edges of the paper over 1" then fold the paper in half lengthwise with the contrasting edge to the outside.

2. Use decorative scissors to cut the folded paper every 1" from the fold to within 1" of the opposite edge. Cut last strip completely from the end and set aside to make handle. Unfold the paper.

3. Punch stars from the folded edges about 1" apart. Glue the punch stars to the strips - one on either side of the center fold, if desired.

4. Roll the paper to bring the ends together, overlapping them slightly then glue in place.

5. Cut edges of paper strip set aside for handle with decorative scissors. Glue one end of the paper strip to the inside of the top edge of lantern and the opposite end to the other side.

Fold paper in half and edges up 1".

Unfold cut paper then roll and glue edges.

$2\frac{1}{2}$"

12"

Bemiss-Jason Fadeless™ Duet Paper;
Fiskars® Paper Edgers and Star Punch; Elmer's® School Glue Gel Stick

Luminaries
by Tracia Ledford Williams

Create fun luminaries using ordinary paper bags. This is a perfect group activity, since you'll want to make more than one for your next party.

You will need:
Pastel colored lunch bags
Paper paint - assorted colors
Stencil sponges
Assorted stencils
Border stencils
Decorative edge scissors
One Votive candle per bag
Hole punch
Sand
Fine tip permanent marker

1. Cut around top of bag with decorative scissors. Punch holes for ribbon then thread ribbon through holes and tie in a bow. Tuck ends of ribbon out of the way.

2. Place stencil on lunch bag. Dip stencil sponge into desired color of paint, then gently tap color into open areas of stencil pattern. Use a different stencil sponge for each color used. Let dry then add details with a fine line black pen.

3. Pour 1" of sand in bottom of bag. Position votive in sand. Make sure ribbons are on the outside of bag before having an adult light the candle.

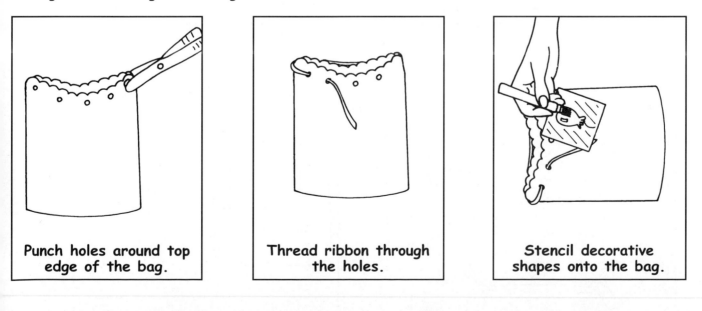

Punch holes around top edge of the bag.

Thread ribbon through the holes.

Stencil decorative shapes onto the bag.

Pillow Talk
by Julie McGuffee for CraftWorks Magazine

What shall we do with all of our wonderful T-Shirts from faraway places and special events? Use them to cover pillow forms for the most unique array of scatter cushions you'll ever see!

You will need:
12" x 12" pillow form*
T-shirt
4 Rubber bands
*The size of the pillow form should be determined by the size of your t-shirt

1. Turn the T-shirt inside out.

2. Gather the sleeves together tightly. Tie them in an overhand knot or secure with rubber bands.

3. Gather each bottom corner and secure the same way.

4. Turn right side out, then place the pillow inside the T-shirt square by pushing through the opening at the bottom. Make sure the T-shirt fits tightly over the pillow form and that the neck opening is turned to the inside. You may find it easier to place the pillow form inside the T-shirt if the plastic cover is left in place on the pillow.

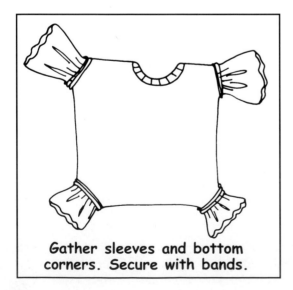

Gather sleeves and bottom corners. Secure with bands.

Turn shirt right side out, then place pillow form inside.

Here's a fun party favor or decoration, filled with candy of course!

You will need:
3mm Yellow, Blue and White foam
70 mm Clear acrylic globe
1½ yds Yellow plastic lacing
Large eye needle
Toothpick
Scissors
Blue fine-tipped marker
Candy
Fishing line
Hanger

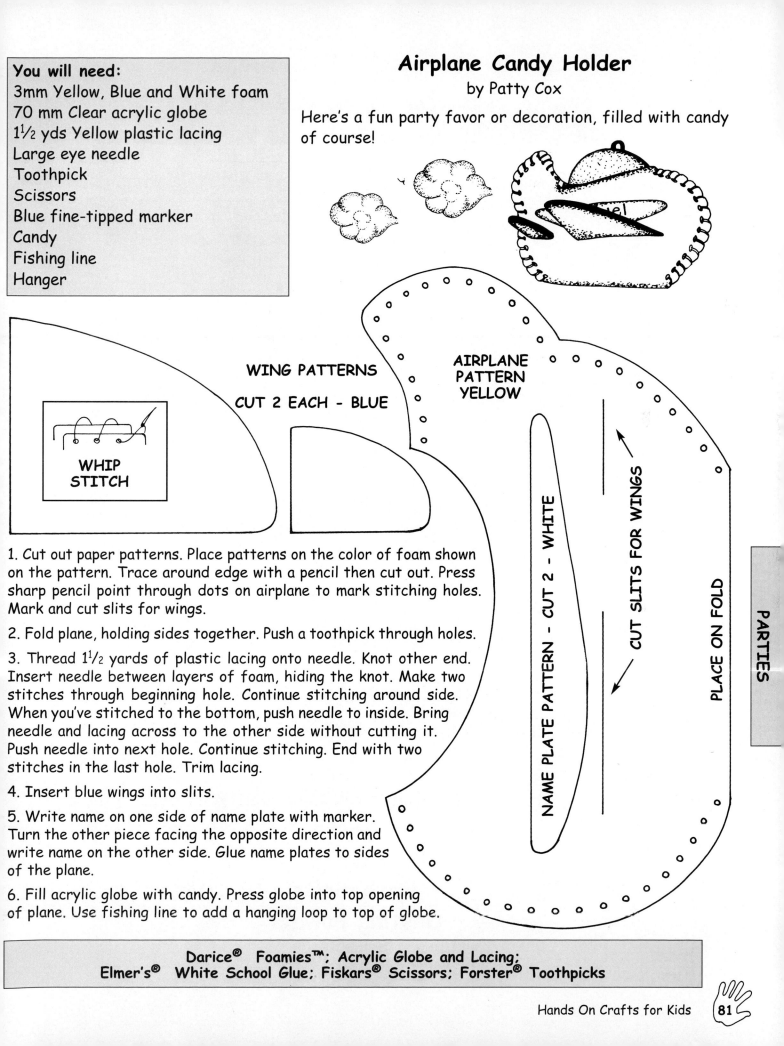

WING PATTERNS

CUT 2 EACH - BLUE

WHIP STITCH

AIRPLANE PATTERN YELLOW

NAME PLATE PATTERN - CUT 2 - WHITE

CUT SLITS FOR WINGS

PLACE ON FOLD

1. Cut out paper patterns. Place patterns on the color of foam shown on the pattern. Trace around edge with a pencil then cut out. Press sharp pencil point through dots on airplane to mark stitching holes. Mark and cut slits for wings.

2. Fold plane, holding sides together. Push a toothpick through holes.

3. Thread 1½ yards of plastic lacing onto needle. Knot other end. Insert needle between layers of foam, hiding the knot. Make two stitches through beginning hole. Continue stitching around side. When you've stitched to the bottom, push needle to inside. Bring needle and lacing across to the other side without cutting it. Push needle into next hole. Continue stitching. End with two stitches in the last hole. Trim lacing.

4. Insert blue wings into slits.

5. Write name on one side of name plate with marker. Turn the other piece facing the opposite direction and write name on the other side. Glue name plates to sides of the plane.

6. Fill acrylic globe with candy. Press globe into top opening of plane. Use fishing line to add a hanging loop to top of globe.

PARTIES

Darice® Foamies™; Acrylic Globe and Lacing;
Elmer's® White School Glue; Fiskars® Scissors; Forster® Toothpicks

MAGIC POTIONS

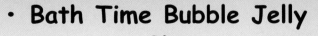

- Bath Time Bubble Jelly
- Glop
- Chalk
- Bath Salts
- Dusting Powder
- Lip Balm

Bath Time Bubble Jelly
by Mary Lynn Watson, Craft House International

You will need:
Packet unflavored Gelatin
¾ Cup water
½ Cup clear liquid soap or
   bubble bath
Fragrance oils
Food Coloring (optional)
Plastic jar with lid (e.g. peanut
   butter jar)
Small plastic bath toy
Mixing Bowl
Assorted items to make label

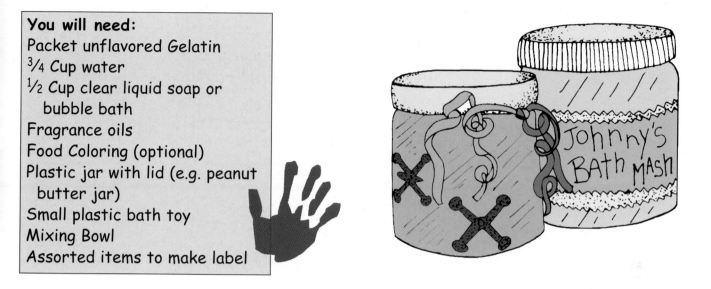

1. Empty the packet of gelatin into a mixing bowl. Set aside.

2. With the help of an adult, warm water until it begins to boil. Immediately remove water from heat source. Carefully pour the hot water into mixing bowl and gently mix with gelatin powder. Allow gelatin to completely dissolve. Be patient! This may take a few minutes.

3. S-l-o w-l-y and gently stir in the liquid soap to the gelatin mixture. Add a drop of food coloring and 5-8 drops of fragrance oil. (Be careful not to beat mixture, bath jelly will become foamy if you do.)

4. Pour your potion into a clean, clear container. Place a small toy inside jar as a treat!

5. Refrigerate Bubble Jelly until set (about 4 hours). As the jelly sets, come up with a name for your creation! Then using scraps of stiff paper and ribbon, make a fun label for the jar. Attach label to bath jelly jar by punching a hole in one corner of the label. Thread ribbon, cut long enough to tie around the jar, through hole on label. Tie around the jar!

6. To use, scoop a small amount of jelly into your hand and hold under warm running water for a bubbly bath-time treat!

Dissolve gelatin in hot water.

Slowly add liquid soap. Do not beat!

Add drops of food coloring and fragrance oil.

Bemiss-Jason Spectra® Construction Paper; Fiskars® Scissors and Hole Punch; Craft House International - 1(419)536-8351

Glop

project provided courtesy of FamilyFun Magazine

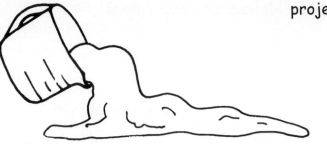

You will need:
8 oz White glue
Food coloring (optional)
1 cup of water
1 tbsp. 20 Mule team Borax

Making "Glop" is fun for all ages! Keep repeating the following process until the glue mixture is all gone. Knead the blobs together and store in an airtight container.

1. Combine glue, food coloring and ¾ cup of water in a bowl.

2. In a separate bowl, combine borax and ¼ cup of water.

3. Add the borax mixture to the glue mixture, stirring until a blob forms.

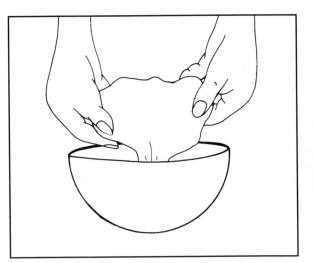

4. Remove the blob. Add another batch of the borax-and-water mixture.

Elmer's® White School Glue

Chalk

project provided courtesy of FamilyFun Magazine

Send a message with your own homemade chalk.

You will need:
Toilet paper tubes
Duct tape
Waxed paper
¾ cup warm water
1½ cups plaster of Paris
2 to 3 tblsp. of Powdered tempera paint

1. Begin by making a mold for the homemade chalk. Cover one end of the cardboard tube with duct tape. Loosely roll up a piece of waxed paper and slip it into the tube. This lining will keep the plaster from sticking to the inside of the mold.

2. Pour the warm water into a disposable plastic container. Sprinkle the plaster of Paris into the water a little at a time until the powder no longer dissolves (about twice as much plaster as water). Stir thoroughly with a spoon then, mix in the tempera paint. To make pastel shades, combine white tempera with a primary color. Rinse your spoon under an outdoor faucet to avoid clogging drains.

3. Place the mold sealed-end down on a level surface and pour in the wet plaster. Lightly tap the sides of the tube to release air bubbles in the plaster. Let the chalk harden for a couple of days. Then remove the tape and slide the chalk out of the mold.

Cover the top of the tube with duct tape.

Insert roll of wax paper.

Pour mixture into mold.

Bath Salts
by Tracia Ledford Williams

Here's a special recipe you can concoct at home then make something special to put it in!

You will need:
Glass suface conditioner
Glass gloss glaze
#18/0 Liner brush
#10 Flat brush
#3/4 wash/glaze brush
Stylus
Black permanent marker
3" x 3" compressed sponge
Epsom salts
Potpourri oil
Food coloring
Masking tape

Teacher Jar:
Glass jar (applesauce jar)
Glass paint - Citrus Yellow,
 Red Red, Apple Candy
 Green, White and
 Shimmers White Frost

Color Block Jar:
Glass Jar (mayonnaise jar)
Shimmery glass paint -
 Blue Ice, Emerald Green,
 Golden Glow and
 Raspberry Sherbet
Glass paint - Silver
 and White

Bubble Bath Jar:
Glass Jar (juice jar)
Shimmery glass paint -
 Raspberry
Glass paint - Fuschia,
 White, Tropical Purple,
 and Silver

Bath Salts:
Place epsom salts in a brown bag. Add scented potpourri oil and a few drops of food coloring and shake.

General Instructions for Jars:
1. Clean all jars with hot soapy water. Rinse well and allow to dry. Brush on surface conditioner and allow it to evaporate.

2. Use stencil sponges for applying blocks of color. Cut the stencil sponges in half lengthwise. Cut these pieces in half and then in half again - eight pieces in all. Clip each piece to the stencil buddy tool and dip into paint to use.

3. Transfer the patterns to compressed sponge. Cut out shapes then rinse in water. Wring out excess water.

Cover surface of jar with surface conditioner.

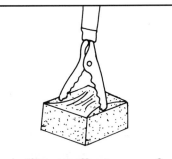

Clip small pieces of sponge to stencil buddy.

Delta® PermEnamels™ Glass and Tile Paint, Surface Conditioner and Glaze;
Eagle® Golden Taklon Brushes

BUBBLE BATH JAR

1. Sponge raspberry paint all over the surface of the jar. Let dry. Apply a second coat if necessary.
2. Use small star-shaped sponge to add silver stars. Use a liner brush to paint yellow, purple and fuchsia hearts between stars. Dip a toothpick into White paint to add trios of dots around jar.
3. Paint lines and dots on center of lid in various colors.
4. Seal surface with an even coat of gloss glaze. Let dry then outline shapes with black pen.

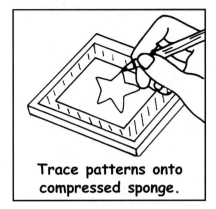

Trace patterns onto compressed sponge.

COLOR BLOCK JAR

1. Paint lid white. Make a masking tape "X" over the mouth of the jar. Run the legs of the "X" all the way to the bottom of the jar. Place a strip of tape around the jar about 1/3 of the way down and another strip a few inches below.
2. Sponge the areas between the taped lines green, raspberry, yellow and blue. Let dry. Remove the tape.
3. Randomly sponge the colors on the lid.
4. Using a liner brush, add white stitch marks.
5. Sponge a large white star on the lid and smaller white stars on the jar between the color blocks. Let dry.
6. Apply a coat of gloss glaze to jar. Let dry.
7. Outline stars with black pen.
8. Add ribbons and a gift tag.

Tape over areas to be left unpainted.

TEACHER JAR

1. Apply two strips of masking tape around the middle part of the jar - one strip about 2" from the top and the other about 1" from the bottom.
2. Sponge red on top and bottom of jar and jar lid. Sponge white on the middle of the jar. Let dry.
3. Sponge red apples around the middle of the jar. Sponge yellow stars between the apples. Paint green leaves with a liner brush. Add a swipe of yellow to the apples to highlight.
4. Add white lettering with a liner brush (123, ABC, 1+1=2, etc.).
5. Use the liner brush to paint a green border around the center section. Use masking tape as a guide. Let dry. Remove tape.
6. Make dots of yellow and green in the red areas with a stylus.
7. Paint center of the lid green. Let dry. Sponge on yellow stars. Make yellow dots around stars. Let dry.
8. Apply a coat of gloss glaze to jar. Let dry. Add details and lettering in the clear section with black pen.
9. Add ribbons and a gift tag.

JAR PATTERNS

Luxurious Lip Balm
by Mary Lynn Watson Craft House International

1. Pour 1/4 cup almond oil into the measuring cup. Place measuring cup in the saucepan of warm water and heat gently. Slowly add 1/4 ounce of beeswax to the warm oil, and wait for the wax to completely melt. (Be careful not to let the water boil out of the saucepan as the wax melts! Add more water to the saucepan, if needed.)

2. Using an old metal spoon, mix the now liquid wax and oil potion together. Flavor the balm by adding five drops of flavor oil. Stir to blend.

3. Remove double boiler with mixture from heat and set aside. Now test the consistency and strength of your lip balm! Pull your spoon out of the blended mixture, allowing a small puddle of balm to remain in spoon bowl. Carefully place spoon in refrigerator to cool. When cool, gently run your finger over the hardened balm mixture. If the Balm is too hard (waxy), add more oil to your mixture. If it is too soft, add more wax. Do this until you've reached the desired consistency. A few more drops of flavor oil can be added at this time if desired.

4. Place double boiler back onto the stove to re-warm and melt any ingredients you may have added. When all ingredients are thoroughly melted and mixed together, have an adult spoon balm into small, clean pots and jars. Set aside to cool. As your balms cool, embellish jar lids with decorative stickers!

Pour almond oil into the measuring cup.

Place measuring cup in saucepan of water.

Pull spoon out of mixture to test balm.

Dusting Powder
by Mary Lynn Watson, Craft House International

You will need:
½ Cup Baking Soda
½ Cup Corn Starch
Old flour sifter or paper bag
Mixing bowl
Fragrance oils
Empty salt shaker
8½" x 11" Paper
Ribbon
Measuring cups
Markers
Scissors

1. Measure equal parts (½ cup each) of baking soda and cornstarch and place in flour sifter. Thoroughly mix the two dry ingredients together by sifting over the mixing bowl. Carefully pour the sifted ingredients from the bowls back into the sifter and repeat this process 2 more times. If you do not have a sifter, you may put the dry ingredients into a zip-lock bag, seal securely then gently shake until the two ingredients are completely mixed together.

2. With the mixed powder back in the sifter, add your fragrance oils. Begin with 5 drops of oil to 1 cup of dried powder. Remember it is always easier to add more scent than it is to take the scent away. Holding the sifter over the mixing bowl, sift the powder and scent together. You will notice when you get to the end of the sifting process that little beads of scent have formed. Using your fingers, gently push the beads through the screen into the mixing bowl with the rest of your powder mixture. Pour the sifted powder back into the sifter carefully and sift the mix into the bowl again. Repeat this step until no more little beads are present. Your powder will then be thoroughly mixed.

3. Roll a sheet of paper into a funnel then secure with a small piece of tape. Hold the funnel over the opening of your salt shaker and slowly pour the powder into the shaker.

4. Decorate shaker with homemade labels. Attach labels with ribbon. Store any unused powder in a zip-lock bag for future use.

Sift dry ingredients over a mixing bowl.

Add a few drops of fragrance oil.

Pour powder into shaker.

Fiskars® Scissors; Craft House International - 1(419)536-8351

Rainstick

by Tim Stull

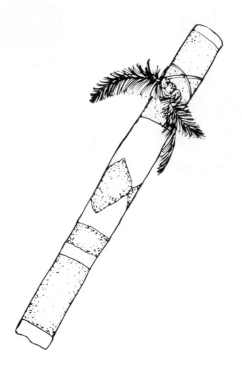

Make this musical rain stick from recycled materials. It's fun to listen to even if you don't want it to rain!

You will need:
Wrapping paper or paper towel tube
Scrap cardboard
Masking tape
12 round toothpicks per 12" of tubing
Cup beads, beans or unpopped popcorn
Nail
Craft Snips or heavy duty scissors
Assorted colors of sand
White no-run glue

1. Trace around the end of the tube and cut two circles from cardboard. Use one to close off one end of the tube. Seal around the edge with masking tape. Save second circle.

2. Use a nail to make small holes next to the spiral of the tube about every inch or less. The length of your tube will determine the number of holes.

3. Stick a toothpick in each hole as far as possible then clip off the end level with the cardboard.

4. Fill the tube with popcorn or beads.

5. Seal the other end with the remaining cardboard circle and tape.

6. Paint one area of the tube with white glue using a scrap of cardboard as your brush. Then roll in sand. Be creative and alternate colors of sand as you paint each area with glue.

OPTIONAL: Decorate your rainstick with leather lacing, beads and feathers.

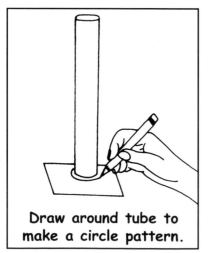

Draw around tube to make a circle pattern.

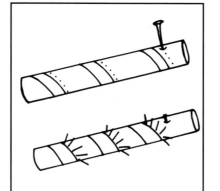

Make holes around tube then insert toothpicks.

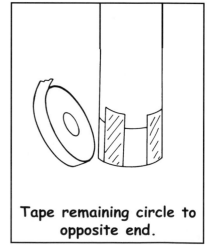

Tape remaining circle to opposite end.

Darice® Sand; Fiskars® Softouch™ Craftsnips;
Elmer's® No Run White Washable School Glue; Forster® Toothpicks

Fiesta Bowl
by Patty Cox

Old newspapers make for a very colorful paper maché bowl.

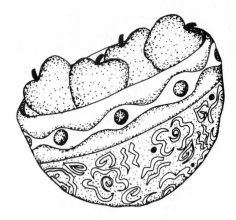

You will need:

Balloon	Newspapers
3" strip of masking tape	Scissors
4½" cardboard circle	Acrylic paints
White glue	Colored Glue
Disposable pan	Markers

1. Cut a 4½" cardboard circle for base. Blow up balloon. Roll a piece of masking tape with sticky side out. Attach round end of balloon to base with tape. Place balloon, tie side down, into a bowl.

2. Cut newspaper into 11" x 1½" strips.

3. Mix 1 part school glue to 2½ parts water in a disposable container.

4. Dip newspaper strips into glue mixture. Squeeze off excess with fingers. Place strip on balloon over cardboard base. Keep adding newspaper strip layers around balloon, leaving only the tied end uncovered. Let dry. Pop balloon and remove. Allow inside of bowl additional drying time.

5. Draw cutting line around bowl top. **Hint:** To make a perfectly straight line, place a bowl on top of paper maché bowl. Draw a line around edge of bowl on maché. Cut along line with scissors.

6. Brush over any loose strips with a mixture of glue and water. Let dry.

7. Paint the outside of the bowl. Allow to dry, then draw designs on the sides of bowl with markers.

8. To make cabochons squeeze dots of colored glue onto a piece of aluminum foil. Allow to dry overnight then peel dots from foil. Glue to bowl sides with dots of glue. Use glue pens to apply colored glue over selected areas of your designs to add dimension.

FLOWER PATTERN

Cover with newspaper strips dipped in glue.

Remove balloon then cut to shape bowl.

RECYCLED

Recycled Pets
by Tracia Ledford Williams

Don't get alarmed by the title, we're recycling containers for pet food and not the pets! Have fun looking for unusual glass containers and jars and scraps of carpet.

You will need:
#6 Flat, #3 Round, and ³/₄"
  Wash brushes
Black permanent marker
Tracing and transfer paper
3" x 3" compressed sponge
Scissors
Glass canisters with wood lid
Glass bowl
Leftover carpet scrap
Acrylic paint - White, Red, Blue,
  Black, Fruit Punch, Yellow
  Orange, and Black
Glass paint - Tangerine, White
  and Red

GENERAL INSTRUCTIONS:
Apply surface conditioner to all glass surfaces before painting. Finish all glass surfaces with a coat of gloss glaze. Let dry. Follow manufacturer's instructions to cure paint.

DOG CANISTER:
1. Basecoat lid white. Let dry. Transfer pattern onto lid. Paint spots black, scarf pink. Let dry. Paint eyes and nose black.
2. Add details and outlines with black pen. Paint pink dots on scarf. Let dry then apply a coat of matte varnish.
3. Transfer bone and heart shapes to compressed sponge, then cut out. Dip in water to expand then squeeze out excess.
4. Sponge white dog bone and red hearts onto the canister. Let dry then add details with pen.

DOG BOWL:
Sponge on white dog bones. Let dry. Outline and add spirals with black pen.

CAT CANISTER:
1. Basecoat lid yellow. Let dry then transfer cat pattern. Paint face stripe orange. Rub cheeks with blush. Paint eyes, nose and mouth black. Paint bow blue and add Pink and yellow dots. Add "Meows" and details with black pen. Paint three blue dots between each word. Let dry. Varnish.
2. Transfer shapes to compressed sponge. Cut out, dip in water and wring out excess. Sponge tangerine goldfish and red hearts on canister. Outline and add details with black pen.

CAT BOWL:
Sponge on tangerine goldfish and red hearts. Let dry. Outline and add details with black pen.

MAT:
Transfer shapes to compressed sponge. Wet and wring out excess. Sponge white bones and red hearts onto mat. Let dry.

Delta® Perm Enamel™ Glass Paint, Surface Conditioner, Gloss Glaze, Ceramcoat® Acrylic Paint and Matte Exterior/Interior Varnish; Fiskars® Scissors; Eagle® Golden Taklon Brushes

PATTERNS

Paint glass surfaces with surface conditioner.

conditioner

Transfer patterns onto compressed sponge.

Sponge shapes onto glass surfaces.

Seedling Pots
by Cindy Gorder

How does your garden grow? Start you own indoor garden from recycled materials and get a head start on the growing season.

You will need:

Empty yogurt cups

Colorful papers - Greens, Purple, Red, Yellow, Orange, Pink, Blue, Brown and Black

Paper crimper

Decorative edge scissors

Scissors

Glue stick

Peat pots

Skewers or craft sticks

Magicraft tape (optional)

Glue sleeve and band around yogurt container.

General Instructions:
1. Transfer the sleeve patterns to colored paper then cut out with decorative scissors. Crimp the sleeve then glue around the yogurt cup.
2. Cut a contrasting strip of paper with decorative scissors and glue it around the middle of the sleeve. Cut and assemble flower and vegetable shapes and glue on the sleeve.
3. To make the markers, write the name of the plant on the appropriate shape and the date it was planted on a second shape. Glue both shapes back to back at the top of a craft stick, or skewer.

Sunflower:
Cut out six yellow flowers. Cut five brown centers with decorative scissors. Assemble four flowers and glue around pot. Glue a skewer between two flower pieces for marker. Glue a flower center on one side.

Cosmos:
1. Cut out two yellow and three pink flowers using decorative scissors. Cut three yellow and two pink centers. Cut a 1¹/₂" circle for back of marker.
2. Make cuts in flowers with scissors. Curl the the edges of the petals around a skewer. Make lots of small cuts toward the middle of the centers. Glue centers to middle of flowers and bend the fringes up.
3. Glue four flowers around pot. Glue a skewer between a flower and the 1¹/₂" circle for marker.

Pansies:
1. Cut six dark purple bottom layers, five light purple middle layers, five dark purple top layers and five yellow centers.
2. Assemble five flowers as indicated. Glue four flowers around pot. Glue a skewer between a flower and the remaining bottom layer for marker.

Peas:
1. Cut out six green pea pods and five sets of light green peas.
2. Assemble five peas. Cut narrow strips of yellow green and curl them around a skewer for tendrils.
3. Glue four peas around pot. Glue a skewer between the remaining two pea pods for marker. Glue peas to one side.

Tomatoes:
Cut five red tomatoes and four green tops. Assemble four tomatoes and glue around cup. Glue a skewer between two tomatoes for marker. Glue a top to one side.

Pumpkins:
Cut two narrow and four wide pumpkins from orange. Cut five green tops. Assemble two wide and two narrow pumpkins and glue around pot. Glue a skewer between the remaining wide pumpkins for marker. Glue top on one side.

Carrots:
1. Cut four orange carrots and three yellow-green tops. Cut fringe in tops. Roll the tops and bend the fringe outwards. Glue to the carrots.
2. Glue three carrots to pot. Glue a skewer between a finished carrot and back for marker.

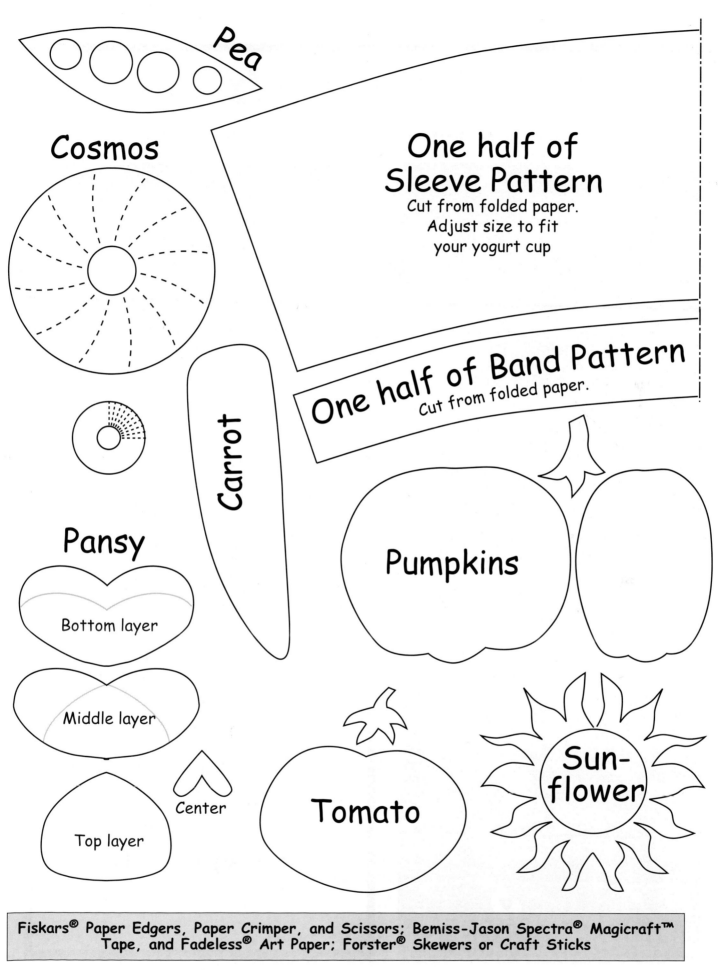

Pea

Cosmos

One half of
Sleeve Pattern
Cut from folded paper.
Adjust size to fit
your yogurt cup

One half of Band Pattern
Cut from folded paper.

Carrot

Pumpkins

Pansy

Bottom layer

Middle layer

Center

Top layer

Tomato

Sun-
flower

Fiskars® Paper Edgers, Paper Crimper, and Scissors; Bemiss-Jason Spectra® Magicraft™
Tape, and Fadeless® Art Paper; Forster® Skewers or Craft Sticks

Add a Figure Jewelry
by Lynda Scott Musante

Make and collect mini figure jewelry. Incorporate birthstones, names and more in these collectible dolls.

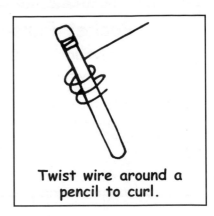

Twist wire around a pencil to curl.

You will need:	
Craft snips	Split ring keychain
Asstd. Colors mini and	Craft wire
regular pony beads	Ruler
Satin cord, or	*Optional*: Birthstone
Plastic lacing	and alphabet beads

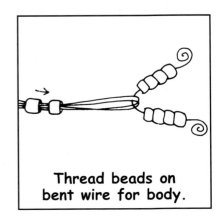

Thread beads on bent wire for legs. Curl ends.

Cut two 6" and two 8" lengths of wire. Bend the 8" pieces in half.

LEGS: Roll the end of a 6" piece of wire around a pencil two times. Slide eight blue beads on wire. Roll up other end of wire with pencil until there is about 1/4" left. Bend wire in half with four beads on each side of fold. Slip the folds of the 8" pieces around the center fold of the leg piece. Slide on two large beads over the four ends of the 8" pieces to form the BODY.

ARMS: Roll the end of a 6" piece of wire around a pencil two times. Slide six beads onto one 6" piece of wire. Roll up the other end of wire with a pencil until there is about 1/4" left. Bend wire in half with three beads on each side of the fold. Wrap center of the arm piece around the body two times. Push the arms down to the top of the body. Slide a large bead on top of arms.

Thread beads on bent wire for body.

HEAD & HAIR: Slide on a large head bead. The four ends of the body wire will become the hair. Twist two ends around the split ring to hold it in place. Curl the ends of all the wires around a pencil. Lightly pull and spread the coils to make hair. Add birthstone, or alphabet beads to hair coils to personalize.

NOTE: be sure to bend the ends of the wire into the coils so that no sharp edges remain.

OPTION: Twist ends around a cord or plastic lacing instead of a split ring to make a necklace.

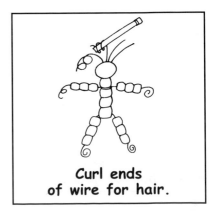

Curl ends of wire for hair.

Darice® Pony Beads, Birthstone and Alphabet Beads, Craft Wire, Split Key Rings; Fiskars® Softouch™ Craft Snips

Hemp Necklace
by Toner Plastics, Inc.

Personalize your wardrobe with a very popular fashion accessory - a beaded, hemp necklace.

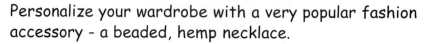

You will need:
4 yards Hemp
2 Wooden beads
Carved oblong bead
40" Strand of hemp
Scissors

Knotting Cords - are 6 times the length of a finished project.

Filler Cords - are 2 times the length of a finished project, plus 8 inches.

BEFORE YOU BEGIN:

1. Determine how long you would like your choker, or necklace to be.
2. Cut knotting and filler cords according to the above formula.
3. Fold each strand in half. (See Fig. 1)
4. To make a loop, fold the looped ends of the cords in an overhand knot ½" from the end. (See Fig.2)
5. Tape the looped end to a clipboard, or other surface. Place a piece of tape over the knot and along the filler cords, adjust placement as needed. (See Fig. 3)
6. Strongly tighten each knot to secure and tie knots as evenly as possible.

To make a 12" choker:

1. Cut one 32" (12" x 2 = 24" plus 8") **filler cord** and one 72" (12" x 6) **knotting** cord.
2. Fold the two strands of cord in half. Tie an Overhand Knot to create a ½" loop.
3. Tie a pattern of square knots that measures 4½" long (approximately 25 knots).
4. Add a wooden bead on the two filler cords then tie 4 Square Knots.
5. String carved oblong bead onto all filler and knotting cords, tie 4 Square Knots.
6. Add another wooden bead as before and repeat the pattern of Square Knots to measure 4½" long.
6. To finish, tie two Overhand Knots and trim ends. To close, push ending overhand knot through the beginning loop.

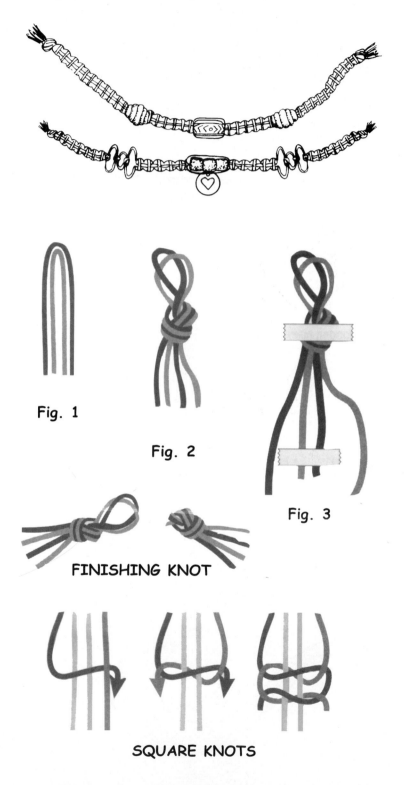

Fig. 1

Fig. 2

Fig. 3

FINISHING KNOT

SQUARE KNOTS

Toner® Natural Knots™ Cool Jewelry Kits; Fiskars® Scissors

ALL DRESSED UP

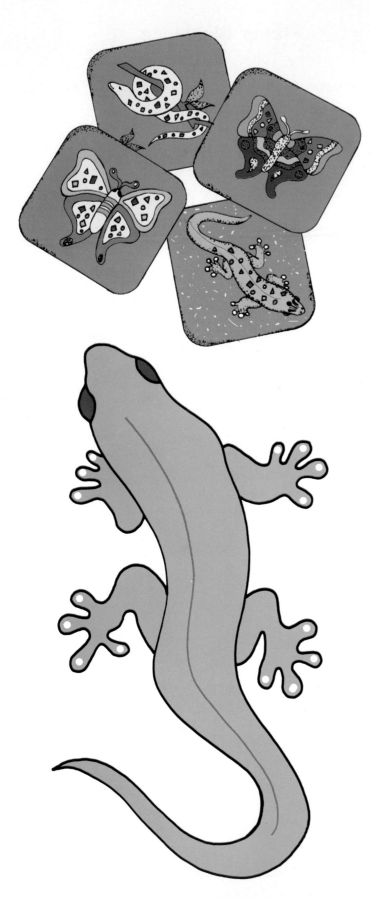

Patches
by Kathleen George

Express yourself with personalized patches to dress up jeans, t's and book bags.

You will need:
Iron-on patches
Acrylic paint - light colors for dark fabric
Liquid Confetti
Liquid Diamonds
Liquid Stars
Small brushes
Tracing paper
Pressing cloth and iron
Drawing paper

1. Trace pattern outlines on tracing paper. Plan the design for your patch inside the outlines.

2. Transfer your design onto the patch using transfer paper.

3. Paint your design using bright colors that show up well on dark fabric. Add white paint to any color that appears thin. You may give some of the colors a second coat.

4. Let the paint dry, then brush with the glitter dazzlers paint. They appear white when first applied, but dry clear. Allow patch to dry several hours. The surface remains a bit sticky until it has been washed a few times.

5. Attach patches only to fabric that can tolerate a high temperature iron. Following the directions that come with your patch, position the patch then lay a pressing cloth on top before ironing. Work quickly - the hot iron could cause the dazzler medium to become very soft if the iron stays on it too long. Peel the pressing cloth away gently. Lay the cloth on the ironing board and press the patch a second time from the wrong side. Follow manufacturer's washing instructions.

Delta Ceramcoat® Acrylic Paint and Dazzlers™; Eagle® Golden Taklon Brush

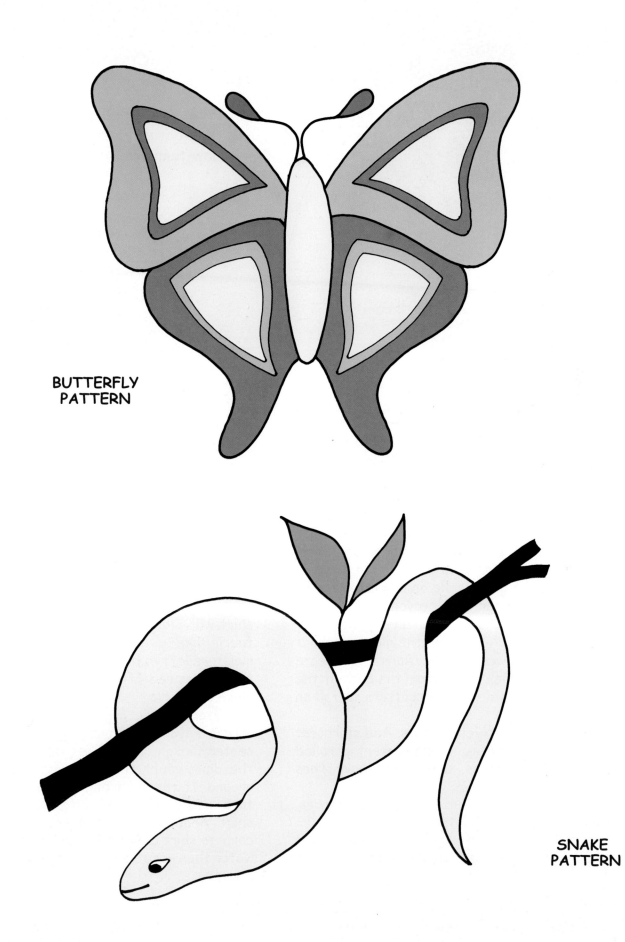

BUTTERFLY
PATTERN

SNAKE
PATTERN

Crayon Batik
by Patty Cox

You won't believe this technique. You actually use soy crayons and a low temperature glue gun to batik.

You will need:
Soybean crayons
Mini lo-temp glue gun
12" x 12" Aluminum foil
Pre-washed T-shirt
Permanent watercolors
1" Flat brush
Embroidery hoop
Newspaper
Optional: Watercolor
      paint crayons

Crayon Batik

1. Lay T-shirt flat on a well protected surface. Open shirt. Center pattern under shirt front.
2. Trace outline of stars on shirt with a yellow crayon. Trace oval border with orange crayon.
3. Remove the wrappers from 3 yellow crayons. Insert one crayon into a mini low melt glue gun. Plug gun in and allow to warm. Place a piece of aluminum foil under tip to catch drips. Place design area of shirt in an embroidery hoop. Place newspapers inside shirt to catch drips.
4. Practice glue gun stroke on a scrap piece of fabric or newspaper. The crayon runs through the tip more sporadically than a glue stick. Allow the crayon to warm in the glue gun about 15 seconds between applications. To create spatters, push the crayon from the back of the glue gun, allowing drips and spatters to fall on the design.
5. Outline and fill in yellow stars. Add starburst lines and an outer wavy line. Insert a rolled newspaper in sleeves then draw wavy lines around each sleeve.
6. Using orange crayon, outline oval border. Draw spirals and add dots.
7. Paint dark blue and purple watercolors over and between crayon design. Allow paint to dry.

Optional: Watercolor Crayon T-Shirt

1. Wet T-shirt then squeeze out excess moisture. Open shirt. Center pattern under shirt front.
2. Trace pattern designs with Payon watercolor paint crayons. The moisture in the shirt will allow the colors to bleed into the fabric like a watercolor. The amount of moisture left in the shirt can vary according to the desired effect. Practice on a scrap piece of fabric.
3. After center motif has been colored, scrape Payon with a straight edge around center design. The flakes will dissolve into the damp shirt creating a speckled background. If the shirt begins to lose its moisture, use a paper towel to tap flakes into shirt. Allow shirt to dry. To add additional color to shirt after it has dried, dip Payon in water then use to add color to shirt. Let dry.

Prang® Funpro™ Crayons, Permanent Watercolors, Payon™ Watercolor Paint Crayons

ALL DRESSED UP

Egg Snowman
by Patty Cox

Styrofoam eggs are the base for these very comical snowmen and cardinals.

SNOWMAN

1. Finely crumble 3 slices of white bread (with crust removed). Add 2 tablespoons glitter gel and 1 tablespoon water. Mix together with a craft stick.
2. Spread mixture on styrofoam with the craft stick. The dough will be sticky. Wet your hands under a faucet, then smooth the dough around the egg.
3. Unbend a paper clip and insert end into top of egg to make a temporary hanger. Hang egg to dry, then remove paper clip.
4. Glue wiggle eyes, pompom nose and E-bead mouth in place. Cut a 5½" length silver chenille stem. Bend into a U-shape. Glue chenille stem and 1" royal tinsel pompoms on sides of head for ear muffs.
5. Spray with clear acrylic finish or paint with a coat of glitter gel and water.

CARDINAL PATTERNS

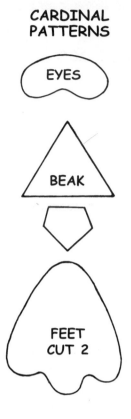

EYES

BEAK

FEET CUT 2

You will need:
3" Styrofoam eggs
3 Slices white bread
Glitter gel
School glue
Craft sticks
Disposable dish
Paper clip

Snowman:
Silver chenille stem
Two 1" tinsel pompoms
Two ¼" wiggle eyes
½" orange pompom
10 black "E" beads

Cardinal:
Red acrylic paint
Red feathers
Black and Yellow foam
Two ¼" Wiggle Eyes

CARDINAL

1. Repeat Snowman steps 1 through 3, using the following recipe: 3 slices white bread, 2 tablespoons red paint, 2 tablespoons school glue and 2 teaspoons water.
2. Allow shape to harden for 30 minutes. Make toothpick holes at wing, tail and top feather placement. Press a pencil eraser into the mouth to make a ⅜" hole. Allow to dry completely.
3. Cut beak, feet and eye pieces from foam. Glue beak in mouth opening. Glue on eye piece and feet. Glue red feathers on body. Glue wiggle eyes on eye piece.

Spread mixture over styrofoam egg.

Use pencil to make holes for beak and featheres.

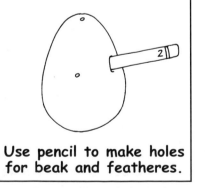

Glue foam beak and feathers in place.

Dow Styrofoam® Brand Plastic Foam; Elmer's® Squeeze Creations™ Glitter Gel, Washable White School Glue; Darice® Pompoms, Chenille Stems, Wiggly Eyes, "E" Beads, Foamies™, Feathers; Delta Cermacoat® Acrylic Paint

Clay Twist Candy Cane

by Brenda L. Spitzer

Striping clay is a great technique that can be used to make many different projects. We start out with a candy cane but stripes can be made into many different seasonal projects.

You will need:
White and Red modeling clay
Decorative glitter glue
Wax paper
Small paint brush
Masking tape
Metallic thread

1. Tape a sheet of wax paper to work table. Break off enough white clay to make a 1" diameter ball. Roll ball between palms until it begins to form a long rope. Place rope on waxed paper. Continue to roll the clay against the table until it is about 8" long.

2. Repeat with red clay. Place the ropes together, side by side. Twist the ropes by rolling to form one striped rope. Place this rope on waxed paper and roll until smooth.

3. Use a knife to cut rope to 5" long. Neatly trim both ends. Bend into a cane shape.

4. Use brush to coat surface of cane with decorative glue. Let dry. Turn the cane over and repeat for back. Let dry.

5. Cut a 12" piece of decorative thread. Tie a loop in the center of the thread around the top of the candy cane in a double knot. Bring the thread ends together and tie with an overhand knot to form a hanging loop.

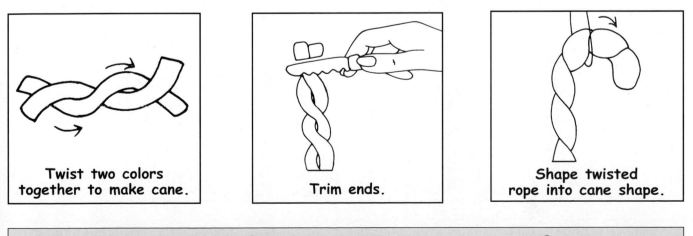

Twist two colors together to make cane.

Trim ends.

Shape twisted rope into cane shape.

Prang™ Modeling Clay; Elmer's® Squeeze Creations™ Glitter Gel; Eagle® Golden Taklon Brush; Fiskars® Ruler and Scissors

COLD WEATHER CRAFTS

Gingerbread House
by Kathleen George

Create this non-edible gingerbread house from paper and styrofoam then fill it with a candy surprise.

You will need:
2 Styrofoam sheets - 18" x 12" x 1"
Styrofoam sheet - 18" x 12 "x ½"
Découpage medium
Brown tissue paper
Brown corrugated paper
Textured craft paper
White chenille stems
Snow medium
Fine glitter
Tuft of fiberfill
Heart shaped beads
Ruler
Utility knife
Tacky glue
2 Wide soft brushes
Scissors
Decorative edge scissors
Wooden skewer
Plastic table knife

1. Cut styrofoam pieces as shown plus the following pieces from 1" thick styrofoam: 7" x 6¾". (back) and 12" x 11" (base). Cut one piece 9" x 4¾" and one piece 9" x 4¼" for the roof from ½" styrofoam.

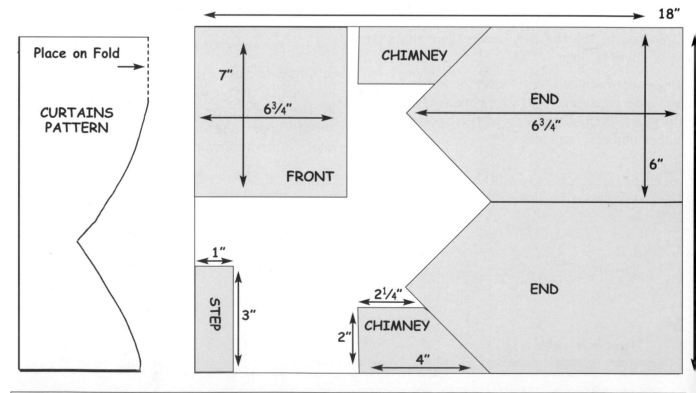

Dow Styrofoam® Brand Plastic Foam; Bemiss-Jason Designer Kolorfast™ Tissue Paper, Spectra® Construction Paper, Waffle Paper, Corobuff™ or Bordette™; Elmer's® Tacky Glue, Decoupage Medium; Delta® Fantasy Snow; Darice® Chenille Stems, Heart Beads

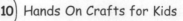

2. Glue ends of house to the front and back. Glue smaller roof piece on the inside of the larger section of roof. Glue the two chimney pieces together.

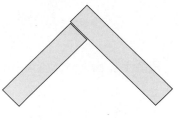

Glue smaller roof piece to larger one.

3. Trace each side of the house on brown tissue paper lightly with a pencil. Cut out about 1/4" beyond the pencil lines. Cut out 1" strips of tissue paper to cover the edges of the roof. Cut an 8½" x 6" piece of tissue for the chimney and a 4" x 3½" piece for the step.

4. Use a wide soft brush to apply a generous even coat of decoupage medium to the surface of one side of the house. Carefully position the tissue paper over the side so that it is centered but not touching the wet surface. Press one side of the tissue down and gently stroke over the top of the tissue with a second dry brush to attach the tissue completely. Use the decoupage medium to glue the excess tissue around the sides and bottom. Leave the top edge unglued. When all four sides have been covered with tissue, allow to dry completely. Then brush a coat of decoupage medium over the top of the tissue. Allow to dry, then cut the excess paper away from the top edge.

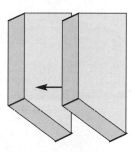

Glue chimney pieces together.

5. Use the same method to glue a strip of tissue over all the edges of the roof and on the front step.

6. Push a skewer or similar tool into the bottom of the chimney so you can hold the chimney easily. Brush decoupage medium on all sides. Wrap the chimney with a piece of tissue so that about 1/2" of the paper sticks out beyond both the top and bottom edges. Let dry. Glue the extra paper down on the top and bottom. You'll need to make little cuts at the four corners so the tissue will lay flat. Give the outside of the chimney a coat of decoupage medium.

Cover roof with strips of scalloped paper.

7. Cover the roof with strips of scalloped corrugated paper. Glue on the lowest strip first, then stagger the scallops of each strip as you glue to the top of the roof. When dry, glue the chimney to the roof.

8. Glue the house to the base. Glue the front step in place. Place the roof on top without gluing.

9. Cut a 2⅝" x 5½" piece of textured paper for the door; two 3¾" x 1¼" pieces of textured paper for the shutters (trim the paper with decorative scissors); one 3½" x 2½" piece of pink paper for the curtains (fold the paper in half and cut with decorative scissors) and a 2½" x 2¼" piece of red paper for the shade (trim the bottom edge with decorative scissors and glue under the curtains). Glue the pieces to the house.

10. Mix 2 tablespoons glitter and 6 tablespoons of decoupage medium. Use a soft brush to paint a thin coat over the roof, doors and shutters to give them a sugary look.

11. Make icing decorations from chenille stems. Glue in place.

12. Use a craft stick to spread fantasy snow on the base around the house. Add a touch of snow to the rooftop, edges and top of the chimney. Let dry.

Curl chenille into icing decorations.

13. Glue a 48" strip of corrugated paper around the edge of the base.

14. Glue a tuft of fiberfil to the top of the chimney for smoke. Punch candy canes into the base at the front corners of the house. Fill the house with candy! Pin extra candy on the roof and along the base if desired.

Winter Candle Holders
by Tracia Ledford Williams

Paint a great face on a clay pot or glass container to bring snow indoors without melting!

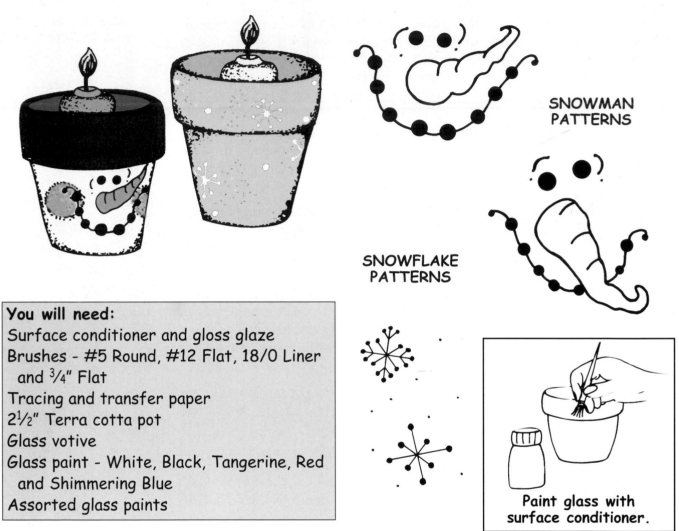

SNOWMAN PATTERNS

SNOWFLAKE PATTERNS

You will need:
Surface conditioner and gloss glaze
Brushes - #5 Round, #12 Flat, 18/0 Liner and ¾" Flat
Tracing and transfer paper
2½" Terra cotta pot
Glass votive
Glass paint - White, Black, Tangerine, Red and Shimmering Blue
Assorted glass paints

Paint glass with surface conditioner.

Apply surface conditioner to entire surface of pot.

Snowman Candle Holder:

1. Paint bottom of pot white and top edge black. Trace, then transfer the pattern on to pot.
2. Mix a small amount of red with white and paint cheeks pink.
3. Paint nose tangerine.
4. Add black dots for eyes and mouth. Use a liner brush dipped in black to add line to mouth and nose. Let dry. Apply a thin layer of gloss glaze to seal.

Snowflake Candle Holder:

1. Paint pot with two coats of blue glass paint.
2. Paint snowflakes white with a liner brush.
3. Apply a coat of gloss glaze. Let dry.

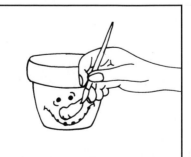

Paint design on pot, let dry then seal.

Delta® PermEnamel™ Glass Paint, Surface Conditioner and Gloss Glaze; Eagle® Golden Taklon Brush